Louisia[na]

ALL THIS IS LOUISIANA

Marguerite Palmer Whitney,
May 1950   White Farms Inn,
Old Lyme,
Conn -

Other Books by

FRANCES PARKINSON KEYES

FICTION

NON-FICTION

POETRY

JUVENILE

ALL THIS IS LOUISIANA

An Illustrated Story Book

By Frances Parkinson Keyes

Photography by Elemore Morgan

HARPER & BROTHERS PUBLISHERS
NEW YORK

TO

DOROTHY GOLDEN MORGAN
AND
ELEMORE MADISON MORGAN, JR.

THE SILENT PARTNERS

IN THE COMPANY

WHICH MADE THIS BOOK POSSIBLE

ACKNOWLEDGMENTS

As I HOPE and believe most readers of this book will realize, it is primarily a recital of my own personal experiences and impressions, which I have felt almost impelled to record, because of the interest and admiration these have aroused over a period of years. Nevertheless, I could not have done this as thoroughly or as comprehensively as my subject warranted, if I had not received a great deal of invaluable co-operation.

In acknowledging this, I should say, first of all, that Elemore Morgan's contribution has gone far beyond the limits of photography. He has taken infinite pains to acquaint me better with various aspects of Louisiana life, of which I previously had only glimpses, but where I had found these glimpses intriguing; and he has suggested many other aspects which I had not discovered for myself and of which no one else had ever spoken to me. Without his suggestions, many entries would have, inevitably, been missing from this book. Among these I should mention iris hunting, coypu trapping, "one-man industries," "lagniappe crops," "peckerwood" mills, the Candle Drill and the significance of sycamores on the batture. Mr. and Mrs. Edward Munson, at whose lovely old home, Glenwood, we made our headquarters while operating on Bayou Lafourche, offered the suggestions which led to our exploration of Grand Petit Bayou.

Besides the persons for whose suggestions I am indebted, there are many others who have co-operated by helping me secure or authenticate material which I knew I wished to include, but which, for one reason or another, I did not find easy to obtain, or concerning which I needed additional information. Among these are Miss Florence Wile, director of the Book Mart in Shreveport, and Mr. R. B. Mahoney of the Shreveport Chamber of Commerce; Mr. Thomas H. Richmond, Jr., director of community activities at Carville; Mr. J. M. Trotter, a prominent rice broker of Crowley and one of my very good neighbors there; Father Henry Holleman, pastor of the Church of the Assumption, Plattenville; Father Eugene Bleakley, assistant pastor of the Church of St. Michael, Convent; Clay Shaw, Managing Director of the International Trade Mart in New Orleans; Mrs. Henry Landry De Freneuse and Mrs. John St. Paul, Jr., president and treasurer of the New Orleans Spring Fiesta Association;

7

Mr. J. F. Guglielmo, principal of the Lutcher High School; Captain George J. Peterson II of the Associated Branch Pilots and many of his fellow pilots; and so many persons connected with the Freeport Sulphur Company that I would find it difficult to enumerate them. This magnificent plant roused my interest the first time I went by its stockpile, platforms and carrier when driving through Port Sulphur on my way to Buras; several years later, I had the pleasure of meeting Mr. A. H. O'Neil, Assistant Sales Manager, at a dinner given by the Carl Pforzheimers in New York; and Mr. O'Neil, in turn, put me in touch with Mr. George Leppert, Assistant to the Vice-President, stationed in New Orleans. My subsequent visits to Port Sulphur and my pleasant sojourns at the staff house have resulted from this chain of events.

The Copolymer Corporation in Baton Rouge and the Chamber of Commerce in Lake Charles have been generally helpful and Mrs. M. L. Clark has helped me unearth antiquated data of various kinds, as she has many times in the past.

I had the great good fortune of visiting the cemeteries of Barataria on "All Saints'" with Glendy Culligan, one of the most gifted staff writers of the *New Orleans Item*. With her permission, I have condensed the feature article she afterward wrote, and re-arranged remaining material in the way that seemed to me best adapted to these pages, correlating it with text of my own. The final paragraph is an abbreviation of an editorial which later appeared in the *Item*. With the permission of Harnett T. Kane, I have quoted his description of Grande Ecaille and his definition of a pilot from *Deep Delta Country*, published by Duell, Sloan and Pearce. Naturally, I am very grateful to both him and his publisher for permission to do so; and I am equally grateful to Ernest Hemingway and Charles Scribner's Sons for permission to quote from *Death in the Afternoon*. The final paragraph in my account of the Rice Festival is adapted from an article of my own, "Louisiana Harvest," which appeared in *Book News*, published by A. C. McClurg in November, 1948; and my account of the Blessing of the Shrimp Fleet at Bayou Petit Caillou is similarly adapted from an article of mine, "This Is My Own, My Native Land," which appeared in *True Confessions* in August, 1946.

Among books of reference which I have found most helpful are *Louisiana: A Guide to the State*, compiled under the general direction of Lyle Saxon, by the W.P.A., and published by Hastings House; *Luxuriant Louisiana*, published by the Department of Agriculture and Immigration; *Louisiana's Natural Resources: Their Use and Conservation*, by John B. Robson, published by Silver Burdett Company; and *Ghosts Along the Mississippi*, by Clarence John Laughlin, published by Charles Scribner's Sons. I have quoted freely from the *Guide;* and the *Ghosts* have been a source of great joy because of their beauty as well as a source of learning because of the careful documentation about them!

In this particular undertaking, I have needed not only detailed information, but the pictures to illustrate it. As I have said in the body of the book—and it is a point which needs stressing—Carnival Balls are private affairs and Carnival Queens would no sooner think of using their pictures commercially than would ladies presented at the Court of St. James. Therefore, it is due to the kindness of Dr. and Mrs. Edmond Souchon and Mr. and Mrs. E. A. Lafaye that I am privileged to use the pictures of their daughters, Dolly Ann Souchon and Beverly Lafaye, together with pictures of the Balls at which they reigned, in this book.* With equal graciousness, Mrs. St. Paul and Mrs. Landry De Freneuse loaned me pictures privately taken at the time of the Spring Fiesta; so these two ladies helped me not only with the text, but with the illustrations. The same is true of Miss Florence Wile, Mr. R. B. Mahoney and Mr. Clay Shaw. Whitney Plantation is not open to the public and, therefore, we are indebted to the courtesy of its owners, Mr. and Mrs. A. M. Barnes, for the pictures taken of its beautiful and unique murals.

* The likeness of Miss Elizabeth Kennard, Queen of Comus in 1949, which appears in one of the pictures of Miss Souchon, is also used by special permission.

Carnival *parades* are, of course, publicly viewed and commercially photographed and so are certain features of the Spring Fiesta. The picture showing the Rex Parade in front of the Boston Club was taken by a staff photographer of the *New Orleans Item*. The photograph showing the Pontalba Building decorated for "A Night in Old New Orleans" was taken by a staff photographer of the *New Orleans States*. The picture of the salt mine on Avery Island was taken by William M. Rittase for the International Salt Company and was made available through the courtesy of this organization; the picture of the pulp forest was made available through the courtesy of the Gaylord Container Company.

These acknowledgments would be incomplete if I made no mention of the debt I owe, in connection with this and all my other work, to the members of my secretarial and household staff. Like myself, they have no English week ends, no forty-hour weeks and not even any regular days off; we all work seven days in the week, not occasionally, but as an established rule, and a twelve-hour working day is by no means unusual. Moreover, supper time is not six or seven or even eight, but when a break comes in the desk work—which may be pretty late and not infrequently is. My secretary of four years' standing, Miss Geraldine Bullock— "Deanie" to all our friends—has borne the brunt of office work; but of late she has been cheerfully helped in many supplementary tasks by the most recent addition to our staff, Mlle. Denyse Claes. My housekeeper, Mrs. Clara E. Wilson—"Miss Clara" to everyone we know in Louisiana—has shown the same steadfastness in her department that has characterized her contribution to my design for living ever since 1930. A tribute to the faithful and devoted service of Creacy and Beverly King appears elsewhere in this book.

—F. P. K.

The Cottage, River Road, 1945
Beauregard House, New Orleans, 1945–1949
Compensation, Crowley, 1947–1949

All the photographs used as illustrations in this book and on the jacket were taken by Elemore Morgan with the following exceptions:

N.B. The photographs illustrating the picking and drying of moss were taken by Elemore Morgan while on an assignment to illustrate an article on this subject for the *Farm Journal*. Through the courtesy of its editors, two prints were withheld from among those taken, in order that we might use them in this book.

     These two pictures were taken by Elemore Morgan for the Esso Standard Oil Company and are used in this book through the courtesy of this company.

TABLE OF CONTENTS

LIST OF ILLUSTRATIONS

Section One—CITY STREETS

Section Two—HIGHWAYS AND BYWAYS

Section Three—FIELDS AND MARSHES

Section Four—BAYOUS

Section Five—THE GREAT RIVER

EPILOGUE

JACKET ILLUSTRATIONS

PROLOGUE

LOUISIANA has many lovers and all of them have sought to extol her. But, because her beauties are so manifold and her attributes so diversified, few have attempted to interpret comprehensively "the infinite variety of her charm." More often, like the admirers of some lovely woman, they have limited themselves to lauding the characteristics which they, individually, have found most appealing. One such suitor will say of his beloved, "She has the brightest eyes in the world," and another, speaking of the same woman, "She has the sweetest voice in the world," and still another, "She has the kindest heart in the world." In like measure, one lover of Louisiana will say, "Where, except in New Orleans, can you find such grille work as there is in the French Quarter?" and another, "Where can you find such hunting and fishing and sailing—in fact, such all round, year round sport—as in the Pelican State?" and another, "Have you seen the Grande Parade of old plantation houses along the River Road? There is no comparable stretch of highway, bordered with so many surviving monuments to living as a fine art." And still another, "Have you eaten crayfish bisque—or buster crabs—or oysters Foch—or wild goose gumbo? No? And you call yourself a gourmet!"

The charming woman, if she is also wealthy, will have some suitors more materially minded than those who speak of her eyes and her voice and her loving-kindness. These will say, "Yes, and besides she is very rich. She is a great land-owner—a magnate's only heiress—a shrewd, successful investor." It is the same with Louisiana. One man will tell you about her oil, another about her lumber, a third will remind you that she is the greatest fur producing state in the Union; and so on. But the man who is an authority on grille work is seldom the same as the one who can appreciate the crayfish bisque, much less concoct it; and the man who seeks to revive lost legends is seldom the one who knows the difference between seed and stubble cane. And so, inevitably, each fails to do Louisiana full justice.

I cannot hope to be entirely successful in giving a more comprehensive estimate of her, but I want to try. For the longer I stay in Louisiana, the more marvels and beauties I discover. And they never pall; they are a source of never-ending wonderment and delight. Moreover, there is an insidious quality to their charm besides that "infinite variety" already stressed. I had no idea, when I first came here, that I should succumb to it: a professional assignment brought me to the Deep South; I was to write a certain novel and then go back to Washington to write another, which I did. But the following year, I seized upon three different pretexts for returning to Louisiana, at three different times; and the year after that I came back to write still another book.

Since then, I have discovered that there is no end to the books which can—and should—be written about Louisiana—indeed, I believe this is one of them! So I am still here. Perhaps I am a little like the man who stopped off, between sailing vessels, in Honolulu, to have his laundry done—and remained twenty years! Or perhaps it is merely that I have drunk bayou water. Once you have done that, so the wisest and oldest inhabitants will tell you, nothing else will ever fully quench your thirst. Therefore, you come back again and again to drink it.

Between such refreshing drafts, I have tried to recall the sights and sounds and scents which have most interested me, most intrigued me and most charmed me. As I have freely confessed, I am only a stranger within Louisiana's beautiful grilled gates, only a wayfarer along her River Road, only an onlooker at her great festivities, only a beneficiary of her rich resources. Perhaps because of this, I should not even try to interpret her. But I would be very selfish if I did not want others to make the same manifold discoveries that I have. So, not as a great sage instructing his hearers, but as a happy wanderer sharing her impressions, I present the following pages, pleased and proud that I can say, in doing so:

"ALL THIS IS LOUISIANA"

Section One

CITY STREETS

NEW ORLEANS

BEAUREGARD HOUSE

IT DOES not belong to me, but to the Beauregard House Association, which rescued it from the ruthless destruction which has robbed not only Louisiana, but the world, of so many architectural treasures. Both Louisiana and the world owe a debt of gratitude to the small group of determined women, led by Mrs. Lydia C. Wickliffe. With far more courage than cash at their disposal, they managed to prevent its demolition to make way for a macaroni factory, and began its restoration. Personally, I am very grateful to them because they have accepted me as a long-term tenant, with the understanding that I would continue the work of preservation and improvement which they had so bravely and so beautifully begun. It is a source of great pleasure and considerable pride for me to welcome friends there; and those who come as strangers to New Orleans feel it is a logical starting point from which to see the city. But first they want to know the story of Beauregard House itself.

I usually begin telling this as we go up the beautiful stone steps, leading from the banquette on Chartres Street to the wide gallery above. For here those divisions which had been Louisiana's proud contribution to the Armies of the Confederacy were reviewed by their erstwhile commander, whom they still loved as their leader: a slender, olive-skinned man, whose hair had turned with surprising suddenness from glossy black to snowy white, but who still carried himself with infinite dignity and whose fine features had infinite distinction: the great Creole, Pierre Gustave Toutant-Beauregard.

There are those who will tell you that this house should not be given his name, because he lived there a comparatively short time. I do not agree; it is not length of time that matters, but significance. However, I am aware that its history did not begin with Beauregard, in the eighteen-sixties, but with Carpentier in the eighteen-twenties and I tell my friends so.

Carpentier was a highly successful auctioneer, with social ambitions and . . .

. . . a beautiful daughter named Telcide. He bought land from the Ursuline Nuns—the first great educators of girls on the North American Continent—and commissioned a leading architect, a Spaniard named Correjolles, to build him an imposing residence opposite their convent. The result was more than gratifying to Carpentier and remains a monument to the memory of the builder. The façade has dignity and restraint. The white paneled doorway leads into an entrance hall seventy-five feet long. On the left are three great square rooms. On the right, the square room at the front leads into another of the same width, but of double length, which was once the ballroom. The Carpentiers moved into their new house and the satisfied auctioneer continued his ascent of the social scale by arranging a very advantageous match for his daughter; Telcide was married off to Alonzo Morphy, a rising young attorney. But since the bridegroom had more prestige than wealth, the young couple continued to live with the bride's parents, occupying the second of the great square rooms at the left of the front door. In due time, a son, Paul, was born to them there. Before he was in his teens, he had become . . .

... the world's greatest chess player.

His genius was discovered quite by accident. His father had been playing with a friend, and after the guest's triumphant departure, Paul, who had been standing by the chess table eagerly watching the game, informed Alonzo that this need not have been lost to the visitor, if a different move had been made. The chessmen were set up again, the game was replayed, and the nine year old child proved his point.

Later on, he was taken on one triumphant tour after another and became the talk of the town and the toast of court circles. But his end was tragic. Trained, like his father, in the law, he neglected the practice of this for his favorite game. Upbraided because of this neglect by the lady he loved, he foreswore chess and turned again to law—only to find that he had lost both his knowledge of it and his knack of interpreting it. He lost the lady too, and died a bitter and broken man, apparently by his own hand. The house on Chartres Street had long since passed from the possession of his family. The sun of the Carpentiers had set. But another was rising.

Shall we go through the dining room to the rear gallery, where we can look out on the courtyard and old slave quarters while we finish the story?

A dashing Creole officer had been the Beau Brummell of New Orleans. Married in his early twenties to a beautiful girl, Laure Villeré, who died shortly thereafter, he had long been inconsolable; when he finally emerged from his mourning, and began to shine again on the social scene, he still evaded the nets laid by scheming mothers with marriageable daughters. He was nearly forty before he married again and then he chose for himself—Caroline Deslonde, one of nine lovely sisters, not unnaturally called the Nine Muses. He took her to the house he had acquired on Chartres Street—this house. It was the scene of an idyllic interlude.[1]

24

Then came the War Between the States. Caroline died. The house was sold. When Beauregard returned to New Orleans he went as a lodger to the place which had once been such a happy home. It is not strange that he stayed there only until he found another habitation. But it has always borne his name—I think, logically. I hope it will always do so worthily.

Yes, there is more to its history than that: stories connected with honest Italian vintners, who made and sold their wines in the basement; stories connected with men who became less honest during the bootleg era, and with men whose wickedness led them to murder on this very gallery. But suppose we leave those other stories for some other time. My study is on the ground floor over there in the quarters and I ought to be back at my desk. The guest rooms are above it and my visitors ought to rest a little. However, I thought that perhaps later on we might stroll down . . .

MY BLOCK ON CHARTRES STREET

. . . Chartres Street towards Esplanade. The four intervening blocks are not among the most important in the city, either architecturally or historically. We see a succession of beautiful wrought-iron balconies, supported on slender iron pillars, but few of the houses which they adorn have imposing proportions and all of them have seen better days. This is now the Italian District and it is not a wealthy neighborhood. Over the passageway leading to the courtyard of a near-by house is a sign with the single word, "HEMSTITCHING," in large letters. Beyond are several small grocery stores, a dry-cleaning establishment, a restaurant. A one-legged man, stationed outside St. Mary's Italian Church, offers pencils for sale, and gratefully receives in his battered hat any small contribution which passers-by offer him. Old women, many of them crippled, sit in the doorways, sometimes calling out to their cronies and sometimes . . .

. . . merely staring into space. Unkempt children dart in and out of dim alleys. Overflowing trash cans litter the sidewalks. Itinerant vendors wheel their snowball carts,[2] ringing their little bells to announce their coming and the youth of the neighborhood comes rushing to patronize them.

Not so long ago, the arrival of a snowball cart, or something similar in character, was about all the neighborhood had to offer in the way of diversion to its youth. But that situation is changed now. And the change came about in a way which I think makes a very touching and inspiring story.

Directly across the street from Beauregard House is the building which is still very generally called . . .

FATHER CARMEL AND THE URSULINE CONVENT

. . . the Ursuline Convent, though these nuns left it long ago for other quarters and, after serving for some time as the Archbishopric, it became the rectory for St. Mary's Italian Church, and the center for the parochial school run by the Missionary Sisters of the Sacred Heart. Constructed in French Renaissance style, it is one of the most ancient and imposing buildings in New Orleans; and though some of its former splendors have faded, it has achieved new power and glory through two Oblate Fathers of Mary Immaculate who live there now.

The elder of these is Father Carmel Gagliardoni, a native of Turin and for many years a pioneering missionary in the Rio Grande Valley. The tales he tells of the early days there have whiled away many hours, when I have been ill. He is gentle and genial, shrewd and tolerant.

FATHER VINCENT AND HIS BOYS

Father Vincent Verderame, Father Carmel's assistant, is also thoughtful and kind about visiting the sick, and the first time he talked with me at any length was one Christmas Day which, except for his call, might have been rather dismal for me. Most of his conversation was about "his boys." For years, he had been conscious of the harm wrought by lack of recreational facilities for the youth of the neighborhood. Just before the outbreak of World War II he had succeeded in raising enough money to build a community center on a vacant lot which had been given him. Then, of course, all building had come to a standstill, except that connected with the war effort. Now that, at last, general building permits were being issued again, the cost of everything had gone sky-high. He couldn't help fearing his boys might have to wait indefinitely for their center.

"And are you a native of Italy, like Father Carmel?" I asked, rather inconsequentially, as he rose to take his leave.

"Me? I was born at the corner of Royal and St. Philip, a couple of blocks from here. These boys I've been telling you about—why, they're just like my own gang!"

Somehow I felt sure Father Vincent would get the money. His singleness of purpose was unmistakable; his conviction of crying need was contagious; everything about him bespoke consecration to a cause. Finally a contractor's sign was posted on the empty lot and a crew of men began to drill and hoist and hammer. Father Vincent's vision had become a reality.

A few months later, he hailed me from the porter's lodge across the street as I was coming down my front steps and asked me if I would not go to the community house with him. From the outset of our acquaintance, it had long been difficult for me to recognize him at a distance as my pastor, for his customary garb—shabby trousers, worn with a green sweater in cold weather, and a frayed shirt, open at the neck, in warm weather—is not outstandingly clerical. But, by this time, I knew him at a glance, so I waved back and said I would be glad to go. As we walked down the block . . .

. . . all the children we met rushed up to greet him; all the old people, sitting in doorways, looked up happily and expectantly at his approach; all the shabby, casual passers-by touched their hats or dropped quick, bobbing curtseys as they said, "Good evening, Father." They were his people, each and every one of them, and they instinctively showed their trust in him and their affection for him.

He took time to respond to every one. But he was still intent on showing me the community house and when we reached it, he threw open the door with pride. Though it was, as yet, unfinished, it was already in use. In the main gymnasium a basketball game was in progress; in a spacious side hall another group was playing ping-pong. A refreshment stand offered Coca Colas and chewing gum. A glass cabinet displayed boxing trophies already won and a large poster gave the schedule of forthcoming matches.

30

"And if it weren't for this," Father Vincent told me in a ringing voice, "they'd all be in the streets, wouldn't they now? Look, the girls are putting on a pageant pretty soon—'Queen by the Grace of God' the name of it is. They have glittery dresses and crowns and everything. You'll come to it, won't you? Wait, I want to show you the showers right now. Lots of these boys, they haven't had anything to wash in before but a pail on the back porch. Do they love those showers! I haven't got the girls' fixed up yet, but that'll be the next thing. We're going to have a benefit performance at the Auditorium, 'People are Funny.' Art Linkletter's coming from Hollywood on purpose. I had to leave out the swimming pool too. But I'll show you the place where it's going to be some day. If the benefit should happen to be a sellout, could be we'd get started on the pool this next summer."

His face shone with the same light that it does when he stands, fully robed, at the altar. And, as if a Voice had spoken them, I seemed to hear the words, "As ye have done it unto one of the least of these my brethren ye have done it unto Me."

ESPLANADE

I believe that when we started our "tour," we were headed toward Esplanade. We are still headed toward it, even though we have lingered a long time—I think with reason—on Chartres Street. Now, let us be on our way.

We are approaching a splendid wide avenue, lined with houses which have retained much of their original beauty and distinction, though Esplanade is no longer the stronghold of the aristocracy, as it was when they were built. Originally a *promenade publique*, it became a fashionable residential center after the glories of the French Quarter, of which it forms the northern boundary, had begun to decline. The Archbishopric was located here for many years, and Chief Justice White was only one among numerous prominent residents. Many of the old families have moved away now, but, fortunately, some have remained and other distinguished persons have come in. The home of Mrs. Louis Perrilliat—a descendant of Governor Claiborne—has been in continuous possession of her family since 1834 and is still one of the show places on Esplanade. The home of Mr. and Mrs. Jan van Tienhoven, beautifully renovated by them, was the bridal gift of Michael Doradou Bringier—one of the wealthiest planters on the River Road—to his beloved daughter, Louise.[3] The imposing . . .

32

. . . residence of the late "Count" Arnaud, the famous restaurateur, has his initials interwoven on the elaborate iron grille work. Through her skillful restoration of a beautiful Neapolitan-style house, Matilda Gray, the prominent philanthropist and archeologist, has performed a great service, both to the immediate vicinity and to the city as a whole.

Among public buildings, the old United States Mint, designed by the famous architect, William Strickland, and built on the site of Fort St. Charles, is another outstanding landmark. It has had an arresting history. Andrew Jackson reviewed his troops here, before the Battle of New Orleans, and William Mumford—the Confederate "martyr" who pulled down the United States flag from the mint—was hanged here. Later it became a Federal jail and during the war it was used as a Coast Guard barracks.

We should not try to hurry along at Esplanade. Its atmosphere is more conducive to a leisurely stroll than to a brisk constitutional. Inevitably, we find it very pleasant to linger under the shade of its trees and pause before its lovely doorways. But when we finally leave it and turn up Decatur Street, an equally pleasant though very different experience awaits us in a ramble through . . .

THE FRENCH MARKET

... the French Market. Its long colonnades of tawny stucco stretch out invitingly before us. They give the effect of that mellowness which comes only with age and this effect is not wholly an illusion: part of the original market, which dates back to 1791, is still intact.

Sheltered by the colonnade and framed by its graceful pillars, the stalls where fruits and vegetables are sold slope backward toward the walls, prismatic in their brilliance. Ranged against the varying greens of lettuce, watercress, escarole, avocados, string beans, podded peas, okra and burr artichokes are the varying yellows of carrots, squash, bananas, grapefruit, oranges and lemons. The purple of eggplant, the red of radishes, strike a still more vivid note; so do the colors of the different berries as they come into season. Coconuts are displayed in their shaggy brown shells, but watermelon are cut open to reveal the luscious pink of their interior. Strings of garlic stir in the breeze, their strong scent mingling with that of sweet-smelling herbs.

I am completely fascinated by these fruit and vegetable stalls. But we must tear ourselves away and go on to the "Morning Call" or the "Café du Monde" to ...

34

. . . drink milk or *café au lait* and eat fresh sugared doughnuts.

Originally designed for the convenience of the teamsters who brought produce to the market, the two cafés quickly became popular with all sorts and conditions of men—and women. Their vogue has increased with the years. Revelers in evening dress make them a last stopping place. Tourists willingly subscribe to the saying that coffee at the French Market will bring them good luck. Career girls save themselves the trouble of getting breakfast by dropping in here. Impecunious teen-agers treat each other prodigally for fifteen cents. Lovers linger over cup after cup, doughnut after doughnut. But none of these has ousted the descendants of the original clientele.

After we have eaten and drunk our fill in this heterogeneous company, we should continue our tour of the market. It grows noisier as we go along and the clamor seems the louder because so many different tongues contribute to its babel. This adds to the sense of confusion we feel as we look at the fish and shrimp brought in from the Gulf, the crayfish and crabs from the sluggish waters of the bayous and swamps, the meats from the plains and pastures—and the people who buy and sell all these things: fishermen, farmers, trappers; society leaders, careful housewives, shrewd merchants; a slum child testing the pinching abilities of a crayfish; a disheartened vendor whose truckload of carrots is still unsold at midnight. And around this same hour, if we have chanced to go there on a Thursday . . .

. . . Roy Alciatore, come to buy fish for the Friday trade at Antoine's Restaurant.

He makes his selections deliberately, noting the brightness of each fish's eyes, the ruddiness of its gills and the resilience of its flesh. He does not patronize any dealer exclusively, but goes from one to another who he knows from experience will prove satisfactory. Among these is Stanley Battistella, who like so many at the French Market, has inherited his business from his father and grandfather. On Thursday nights Stanley always has a good supply of pompano on hand, awaiting Roy's inspection; he knows they will be greatly in demand for *pompano en papillotte* next day.

Pompano are not sold by weight but by fish; however, Roy finds it easy to gauge the weight and knows that a two-pounder provides two portions. He usually buys about fifty pompano at a time, unless he is preparing for a big party at which this specialty will be featured—when, of course, he buys more. As a rule, he has these loaded in his own car and takes them back to the restaurant himself. Then they are cleaned and put in a refrigerator to remain until orders come through for them. When this happens . . .

37

ROY AND HIS RESTAURANT

. . . one of the chefs, very probably John Daigle, removes the pompano from the refrigerator, filets it, skins it, and poaches the filets in white wine, vinegar and herbs. Next the sauce, or *roux*, is prepared, the water in which the fish has been boiled—the *velouté de poisson*—being used as a moistening agent for the flour as it is browned in butter. Green onions, bay leaf and thyme go into this sauce, and finely minced shrimp and crabmeat, already sautéed in butter. While this sauce cools and hardens, a heart-shaped piece of parchment paper, well oiled, is carefully spread out and alternate layers of sauce and pompano placed upon it. Then it is folded, closed and re-oiled; and finally it goes into the oven from which, half an hour later, it is solicitously removed by the waiter who has taken the order for it.

When I first came to New Orleans as a writer, one of my best advisers cautioned me that I would get much better service, at all restaurants, if I experimented until I had discovered the waiter who seemed best suited to my special needs and then made it a point to ask for him always. My choice fell upon . . .

. . . Albert Feugas, whose own history, which I have learned partly from him and partly from others, is so interesting that I think I should interrupt my chronicle of a pompano's progress to tell it here:

Albert was born in a Pyrenean village where his father was the innkeeper. At the age of twelve he was apprenticed to a local barber, whom he left in order to study the art of wig-making in Bordeaux. It was as a wig-maker that he came, while a very young man, to New York; but almost instantly he abandoned this trade—"Just like all you Frenchmen!" as his irate employer exclaimed—and went as assistant to the second cook at the old Lafayette Hotel, whose demolition is still a matter of such poignant regret. The climate "drove him south." He betook himself to New Orleans, applied to Jules Alciatore—Roy's father—for a job and was again "put behind the range." But his submerged talents as a super-waiter somehow made themselves manifest and he was moved to the front of the restaurant, where he remained until early August, 1914. Then, with six hundred other Frenchmen, he set sail for France. Not one of these men had been called out under French military law. Every one was a volunteer.

That all these loyal sons of France served their mother country valiantly I do not for a moment doubt; but certainly very few earned and received the signal honors that came to Albert. The war had been going on only a little over two months when he won his first citation—for volunteering to lay wires within twenty-five yards of the German lines. He saw continuous service, except when hospitalized, up to the very eve of the armistice; at that time he was incapacitated by his fifth wound. Meanwhile, he had been awarded the Médaille Militaire and the Croix de Guerre with seven citations, each for some exploit more daring than its predecessor. At the end of the war when he returned to New Orleans, he was named a Chevalier of the Legion of Honor. In this capacity he attends those exclusive functions at which members of the Order are the special guests. (The latest of such functions at which I happened to see him was a luncheon given at Arnaud's in honor of the Ambassador of France, Monsieur Bonnet.) But, except on the occasions when such events are celebrated, and on Sundays, when Antoine's is closed, he is on duty as a waiter at the century-old restaurant.

He presents each dish not only with an air of deference to the diner, but with an awareness, amounting almost to reverence, of the art that has gone into its making. In the case of *pompano en papillotte* the technique is very delicate: holding the plate on which it is served firmly in place with one fork, Albert runs another down the center of the parchment paper, which is now browned and brittle. Next he folds first one side and then the other of the paper so divided back over the fork with which he has made the incision, deftly withdrawing his instrument afterward. Then he stands back for a moment, smiling with satisfaction as his patrons take their first mouthful. There is no reason for haste. The long loaves of crisp, hot bread, wrapped in a spotless napkin, are already on the table. So is the old-fashioned carafe which—unless flowers have been specifically ordered—forms the invariable centerpiece at Antoine's. The water glasses have been filled from it. Presently Albert will fill the wineglasses too, from the bottle which has been set to cool by the table; and, unless the hostess has already arranged for the menu, he will make unobtrusive suggestions as to what might suitably follow the pompano and the Montrachet. *Filet de Boeuf Marchand de Vin? Pigeonneaux Paradis? Soufflé Surprise? Omelette aux Confitures?* He nods his understanding interest and leaves the room, quietly closing the door behind him.

Roy Alciatore has been offered fabulous sums to open branch restaurants in various parts of the country. His answer is always the same, "There can be only one Antoine's." No one who has had the privilege of acquaintance with the restaurant will challenge the accuracy of this statement—especially after eating *pompano en papillotte,* served by Albert Fuegas, Chevalier of the Legion of Honor.

MAISON DE VILLE

Antoine's Restaurant is on St. Louis Street, about halfway between Royal and Bourbon. When I have eaten lunch there, I like to go on to Bourbon, turn right, and walk a block to Toulouse—because, by turning right again there, I come almost immediately to four establishments, very different in character, each of which has its own special fascination for me.

The first of these is the so-called Maison de Ville, an erstwhile private residence which has been transformed into a small, exclusive and utterly delightful hotel. Its transformation came about in this way:

During 1944, a Pennsylvanian by the name of Madeline Erlich paid her first visit to New Orleans and was both astonished and disappointed to find that there was, in the Vieux Carré, no hotel which had deliberately sought to preserve or re-create the unique atmosphere of this famous quarter, in the same sense that a similar thing has been done in Central City and San Antonio—to give only two familiar examples. In the course of her visit, she made the acquaintance of Mrs. A. W. McDougall, the director of a successful travel bureau, and enjoyed the hospitality of the McDougall home on Toulouse Street. Here she "saw a patio for the first time," and learned that the property had once belonged to the famous apothecary, Antoine Amédeé Peychaud, whose curative bitters are still on the market, but whose renown rests more securely on the fact that he is credited with having invented the cocktail!

The beauty of the place charmed her and so did its history; and in the congenial atmosphere created by the McDougalls, she eventually summoned courage to voice her disappointment because the Vieux Carré had no "typical" hotel. The McDougalls agreed that the lack should be remedied. But a prolonged search led to nothing that seemed suitable for their purposes, and finally Mrs. Erlich made a bold suggestion: would the McDougalls consider moving to a smaller house themselves and converting the one on Toulouse Street to the uses the two ladies so clearly visualized and so urgently desired?

The McDougalls would—and did. They found an equally charming, but smaller place on Governor Nicholls Street; and while both houses were being remodeled, Mrs. Erlich undertook the task of assembling furniture and decorations for the Maison de Ville, of which she had consented to become the manager. Among her "finds" was a door from the famous St. Louis Hotel, whose virtual destruction by the hurricane of 1915 was regarded as a disaster by hundreds who admired its architectural magnificence and revered its great traditions. This door, in which a panel of etched glass is set between two sections of exquisite carving, opens into a small hall, flanked on one side by Mrs. Erlich's own quarters and on the other by the first of the twelve guest rooms, each faultlessly furnished in ante-bellum style. Beyond are a small office and a pleasant lounge, where continental breakfasts are served. But the visitor begins to get the real "feel" of the place when the rear door is opened into the . . .

. . . patio.

It is paved with mellow brick and surrounded by blossoming trees—oleander, mimosa, camellia, Jerusalem thorn. In the center stands an old well, encircled by flower beds. The garden furniture is modern for the most part, but it does not strike an incongruous note. Supplementing it are several old school benches, conveniently placed behind marble-topped tables for which the iron framework of old sewing machines forms the support. (I have seen similar tables used elsewhere in Louisiana and they are extremely effective.) The old *garçonnière* runs along one side of the patio, and in this part of the building the guest rooms have been furnished in somewhat simpler style than those in the main house, with the idea that they would thus be more in harmony with their original use; but they are all charming and they are all provided with every convenience. The guest rooms at the rear of the main house also "give" on the patio and the encompassing balconies are as intriguing as they are serviceable. Beyond a garden gate at the rear is the famous Court of the Two Sisters, to which the delightful patio of the Maison de Ville seems like a natural antechamber. The visitor who enjoys Café Society can have it simply by going through this gate. On the other hand, the visitor who prefers quiet and solitude may remain in the patio, resting after happy wanderings and before undertaking others, or indefinitely idling pleasant hours away.

> "No dream endures until a distant day
> Unless it falls a thousand times to earth. . . ."

Madeline Erlich has made her dream come true. I know that she is the happier for it, as is every woman who realizes a vision. Moreover, I think that she has made a very great contribution to the revival of the French Quarter and to the enjoyment and comfort of many who come to see it.

Just a little farther down Toulouse Street lives another woman who has made a different, but equally significant contribution to the atmosphere of the Vieux Carré. This is . . .

MRS. HOVEY-KING AND HER PERFUMES

. . . Mrs. Hovey-King, whose house, the so-called Casa Flinard, is one of the finest examples of early Spanish architecture in the city. As the wife of a Naval officer, Mrs. Hovey-King traveled and sojourned in many different parts of the world and, in the course of her wanderings, became deeply interested in the art of perfumery, as this is practiced in the South of France, in the Orient, and elsewhere. For her own enjoyment, she began to experiment in mixing precious oils and essences and, after her husband died, it occurred to her that she might put these experiments to both pleasant and practical use. The many fragrant plants indigenous to Louisiana offered a natural inducement to specialize in these: magnolia, sweet olive, gardenia, oleander, vetivert—who could ask a more provocative chance for selection? She decided to turn the ground-floor drawing room of her house into a perfume shop and the dining room behind it into a laboratory; the second story of the Casa Flinard was spacious enough to provide comfortable and attractive living quarters; and beyond the entrance was a patio, reached by a domed driveway, which would be an asset to both private and professional living.

The plan has worked out to perfection, not only from the practical but from the artistic point of view. A small bay window, invitingly stocked . . .

. . . and decorated, arrests the attention of the passer-by. A Siamese cat, Lightning, whose habit it is to move circumspectly about among the fragile flacons, adds greatly to the decor. She regards the onlooker with condescension, if she deigns to regard him at all. "It is nothing to me whether you buy perfume or not," Lightning seems to declare. "I am settling myself for a snooze. Do not disturb me."

In spite of the cat's detachment— or possibly, because of it—the stroller, his entrance heralded by the soft tinkling of a bell, is soon inside the exquisitely appointed shop. He pauses to admire the pastel-colored paneling and the delicate French prints as he does his leisurely purchasing. Then, like as not, he will fall in with Mrs. Hovey-King's hospitable suggestion that he might like to see more of the Casa Flinard—and he will be wise if he does, for he will find in it much to admire. Its cypress timbers are hand-hewn and hand-tooled; its iron hinges and latches are hand-wrought; its stair railing and mantels are hand-carved and all its antique furnishings are in complete harmony with their noteworthy setting. It will be some time before he leaves, his package of perfume under his arm and then, almost immediately, he will come to a halt again before . . .

THE PLANTATION BOOK SHOP AND THE
EDMONDSON ANTIQUE SHOP

. . . the Plantation Book Shop and the Edmondson Shop of American and English Antiques.

Of course New Orleans abounds in book shops and antique shops. Royal Street is especially famous for the latter, and almost everything that a connoisseur could covet may be found there in a suitable setting and amidst elegant surroundings. There is no city with which I am familiar where antiques are more tastefully and lavishly displayed than in those establishments of New Orleans which cater to the luxury trade. But, personally, I prefer the smaller and less pretentious ones—especially those where some of the wares are set out on the sidewalk. Sometimes this is done because the little shop is itself so crowded with "trash and treasures" that its director needs to take advantage of the easiest means to expand; sometimes—I suspect—because he realizes that samples thus readily viewed serve as the wiliest possible means for luring a prospective purchaser inside to see more. But the motive is unimportant to me. I am so fascinated with the result that I seldom succeed in withstanding the temptation into which I have been led; Mrs. Edmondson presents this to me in many enticing forms. Though magnificent specimens of English antiques are probably the most valuable items she offers, her own penchant is for fine porcelain, particularly porcelain figurines. It is nothing short of miraculous that I have not been persuaded to decorate every mantelpiece in Beauregard House with such fragile *objets d'art.*

What is true of antique shops is even truer, in my case, of book shops; I can no more be trusted to get by one than an inveterate drunkard can be trusted to get by a bar. And when a book shop is run, as the Plantation is, by persons like Mr. and Mrs. Harold Leisure, my fate is sealed in advance. For, they are not merely booksellers, they are bibliophiles themselves. The . . .

48

. . . original nucleus of their stock was their own private library; and every addition to it has been made with feeling and knowledge. They have the latest novels available for those customers whose taste runs in that direction; but they also have available both the shabby little secondhand volumes of poems and the beautifully bound examples of belles-lettres which appeal to entirely different types of customers. Unfortunately, perhaps, I fit into all these categories with the greatest of ease. I love books as such—the feeling of them, the sight of them, the smell of them, no less than their contents. Even if I have left Antoine's just after lunch, it is quite likely to be getting dark before I am ready to leave my favorite haunts on Toulouse Street.

If it is, I go back to Royal Street again, in order to pass by . . .

49

ST. LOUIS CATHEDRAL AND PÈRE ANTOINE'S GARDEN

... the rear of St. Louis Cathedral. This is not the best-known view of it. Most persons prefer its façade, as seen from Jackson Square, with the sun shining brightly upon it. But the aspect which seems to me most significant is the one it presents after nightfall, when the great white statue of Christ, with arms outspread, casts a shadow in the shape of a cross on the wall behind it and the green plot in which the statue stands is veiled in darkness.

The green plot is known as Père Antoine's Garden, and deepening twilight enhances the mysterious charm with which it is imbued at all times. Père Antoine—or Fray Antonio de Sedella, to call him by his real name—was a Spanish Capuchin who came to Louisiana in 1781, became pastor of the Church of St. Louis—now St. Louis Cathedral—and several years later was appointed Comissary of the Inquisition for Louisiana. The colonial governor, Miro, sensed the potential danger of this appointment and adroitly managed to have the Capuchin seized and deported. But, after Miro was replaced in authority, Père Antoine returned and, a controversial but beloved figure, served as parish priest until his death in 1829.

Many legends cluster around his name. According to one of these, he and his great friend, Emile Jardain, while preparing for the priesthood together, fell in love with the same girl—who eloped with Jardain. Years later, he deserted his wife and, on her deathbed, she sent her baby to Père Antoine. He did his best for it, but the baby died too and Père Antoine planted a palm tree to mark its little grave. Ever since, the palm tree has grown and flourished and brought forth abundant fruit.

Père Antoine's Garden, however, has not always been respected as a holy place. According to another story, nearly all the duels fought over the girls who graced the Quadroon Balls took place here. Gay young bloods did not ...

... wait to go out to the Dueling Oaks, where City Park is now located, the morning after a dance, if two of them wanted the same girl. The Orleans Ballroom was only a stone's throw from the Cathedral. It was much simpler to settle the question of conquest at swords' or pistols' point immediately. The survivor of the duel got the girl. It was as simple as that. Perhaps Père Antoine, who had been thwarted in his own love affair, looked with a lenient eye on those who dealt more directly with such matters than he had. It would not be strange if his tragic experience had given him tolerance; it often happens so. And, somehow, the statue of Christ seems appropriately placed here. Not only because of its proximity to the Cathedral; but because of its proximity to the problems and the passions of life and to the scene of sudden and violent death.

JEAN LAFITTE'S BLACKSMITH SHOP

Unless the visitor to New Orleans is exceptionally austere or exceptionally high-brow, he will feel that his sightseeing is incomplete if he does not go up and down Bourbon Street, after nightfall, for a survey of its attractions.

At almost every other door, sounds of revelry will stream out to greet him and he will be arrested by a dazzling poster and a neon sign, even if he has not already been hailed by a persistent and vociferous barker. He can go straight from one place of amusement to another close by. According to one of my friends, Bourbon Street is the only one of its kind left in the United States now that the Barbary Coast in San Francisco has been transformed. This same friend maintains that there is much genuine talent on Bourbon Street, not a sorry imitation or a canned variety of it. I am quite prepared to agree. Jazz originated in New Orleans, as well as various other unique and vital forms of self-expression which have enlivened millions.

Candor compels me to admit that my own dancing days are over, and that, even before they were, I was not much of a night clubber, in the usual sense of the word. However, I do have a favorite haunt on Bourbon Street . . .

. . . a small ancient structure of *briquete entre poteaux,*[4] quaintly out of keeping
with its garish surroundings. It is flush to the sidewalk on the corner of St. Philip;
but a pleasant terrace, shaded with banana plants, flowering shrubs and a large fig
tree, separate it from the tall building on its south side. It is still known as Lafitte's
Blacksmith Shop, for, according to legend, this is the place where Jean and Pierre
Lafitte posed as blacksmiths while actually engaged in carrying on the flourishing
slave trade, which they designated as "dealing in black ivory." But it is now run as
a bar. In summertime, small tables are set out on the terrace in the evening and the
cool breeze stirs the encircling boughs and branches; it is very pleasant to sit there and
sip an iced drink after a long day's work. It is equally pleasant, on a winter night, to
draw a chair up close to the great stone fireplace inside and savor a hot toddy. . . .

I am beginning to realize that I have kept my visitors for a long while in the
Vieux Carré; that is because I am so fond of it myself that it is hard for me to
leave it. It is high time we started uptown. But before we do, I have a special reason
for wanting to cross over St. Philip to . . .

CORALIE AND HER FAMILY

. . . Dauphine Street.

There is nothing about it, at the present time, that suggests a crown princess of France, though doubtless there was when it was so named; and there is nothing about the beauty salon of Coralie Ragus that suggests establishments which cater to feminine vanity in Paris, though its title was, undoubtedly, prompted by the ambitious hope that it might. For Coralie is nothing if not ambitious; she is also excitable, voluble and quick tempered. And, incidentally, she is one of the best hairdressers I have ever discovered since the golden days of Vienna.

Coralie was first recommended to me by a lovely lady whom I questioned about the possibility of finding a hairdresser who would come to the house. I was then living on upper St. Charles Avenue, working intensively on *Crescent Carnival,* and I could not take the time to go downtown to a standardized beauty parlor. So, I got in touch with Coralie and she came to me—not as often as I would have liked, for it appeared that she or some member of her family was frequently involved in some extraordinary crisis which prevented this; and not very promptly when she did come, because, apparently, some lesser crisis always delayed her at home, just when she was ready to leave; or else the streetcar she took broke down, unless the one she meant to take did not run at all; so that she had to take a taxi and the Holy Mother knows, according to Coralie, that you can never get a taxi when you need one. But, eventually, she did get there, and before she left, my hair was clean and curled and orderly, and, as she darted out of the door, I realized that an element of great vitality, coupled with great talent, had gone with her.

Later, when I moved down into the Quarter myself, I told her I would come to her; and presently I discovered further evidences of that vital talent. In a crowded row of drab houses, Coralie's shone with fresh paint and even the front doorsteps were waxed; while at the side a well-tended garden was bright with every conceivable sort of bloom. I never saw Coralie's garden when it was not blossoming. The beds have scalloped borders, and garden ornaments in the form of herons, swans and globes are carefully disposed on the strips of lawn at the most effective intervals. An iron fence, glistening with aluminum paint, forms the enclosure.

Coralie is proud of her garden, as well she may be, though I suspect that the house, which is in a constant state of upheaval because of improvements and reorganization, means even more to her. It used to be a neighborhood center crowded with gossipy women who brought their noisy children with them, boys and girls chasing their undisciplined pets, and gum-chewing bobby soxers whose gangling "dates" wandered casually in and out. Now, it is much more exclusive. In fact, the Parisienne Beauty Salon is open only on alternate days, because on the other days Coralie is busy looking after the apartments she rents and making herself useful to the Sisters of the Blessed Sacrament, who operate Annunciation High School, which Coralie's daughter, Jackie—Jacqueline—attends on a scholarship.

And one year, Jackie . . .

. . . was elected Queen of Carnival there.

It is a mistake to suppose that it is only to a debutante of exalted social standing, whose parents are either very wealthy or willing to forego all other luxuries, that such an honor can go. The love of Carnival is an integral part of the Louisiana character, irrespective of class distinction. The determination to have a part in it, the bigger the better, is frequently one of the earliest traits to make itself manifest in a small child and one of the last to diminish with old age. When it comes to teen-age queens, these are even more numerous, though far less heralded, than debutante queens. I am told that there are two hundred and fifty schools in New Orleans alone, not to mention Lafayette and many smaller cities. Jackie's election, preparation and reign are all typical of what goes on in dozens of similar cases.

The society girls normally select the fabulous costumes which cost thousands of dollars from establishments that specialize in such luxuries; in most cases, the teen-ager, attending a public or parochial school, can do nothing of the sort. But it is not necessary that she should. Her election has been a matter not only of family but of community pride; her aunts and cousins, her next-door neighbors, the folks who live just around the block—all these want to have a hand in her adornment. For eighteen nights before the ball at the Annunciation High School, a group of women gathered around the dining room table and sewed sequins on Jackie's crimson velvet mantle. A wide border of sequins surrounded it; a giant bird and a huge bow and arrow were patterned halfway down its immense length; in all, no less than forty-five thousand sequins were painstakingly sewed upon it by hand; and a correlative design of sequins was also sewed on the front of the lace-frilled, white velvet dress which rested in snowy splendor on the sheet covering the table after the mantle . . .

. . . had been finished and spread out in all its magnificence, almost completely covering the parlor floor. The needlewomen, their eyes aching and their fingers sore, but their hearts throbbing with pride, clustered about in little groups, gazing down on their handiwork. Their hostess' son circulated among them, passing Coca Cola and himself casting covert, but admiring glances in the direction of the mantle.

The occasion assumed a more and more festive character; a dress rehearsal seemed to be indicated. Coralie and Jackie retired, bearing away with them the snowy dress and the shining mantle. The chattering groups subsided into expectant silence. Then Jackie came back into the room.

A few minutes before she was dressed in a pleated skirt, an unbelted Russian blouse and the inevitable white socks. Her shoes were scuffed and her curls tumbled over her shoulders. She walked with a slouch and chewed gum. But now . . .

. . . she was completely transfigured. She had a glittering crown on her upswept hair and a glittering sceptre in her hand. She wore her royal robes as if she had been born to the purple and advanced with perfect poise. Her smile was cordial but composed. Her splendid dark eyes reflected the happiness of those around her. Her shoulders were soft and white, like the lace which veiled them. There was something breathtaking, though less about the sudden transformation than about the youthful beauty and grace so unexpectedly revealed.

The following evening she was still more dazzling.

The Carnival Ball was held in the auditorium of the Annunciation High School. This auditorium is situated on the third floor, which involves quite a climb; and, in the course of it, as we paused for breath, we caught glimpses of several religious statues, surrounded by small twinkling lights, which adorned the various hallways. The auditorium was packed. Proud parents had turned out in full force and occupied seats at the right of the center aisle. Those on the left were reserved for the Sisters of the Blessed Sacrament, who filed in together, their Superior at their head. At one side of the hall were ranged all the Annunciation girls who were not taking part in the pageant. The other side was left free for exits from the stage, where the curtains remained drawn. An orchestra was busily engaged in rendering, "Let Me Call You Sweetheart, I'm in Love With You." As this air was repeated over and over again before another was rendered, I concluded that it was a special favorite.

The first part of the pageant was enacted at floor level, with the drawn curtains as a background. The theme was the story of Hiawatha, and wigwams, campfires, a war dance and a tribal wedding were all realistically featured. Then came the pause which signified the imminent appearance of the queen. The door at the left of the stage opened and Jackie came down the steps, with the same smiling poise which she had so suddenly assumed the evening before. Her sceptre was concealed by the large bouquet of red roses which she carried. When she reached the group of nuns, she paused in her royal progress and, bending over, kissed Sister Mary Aloysia while handing her the roses. Then the procession continued.

One by one, the maids followed after the queen. The stage curtains parted at last, revealing the throne and the waiting king, who advanced to meet his consort as she finished her progress around the hall. The knights and pages took their proper places and presently general dancing began. From beginning to end, the proceedings had moved smoothly and efficiently and the tableau would have been a credit to any organization. But somehow we felt that it was not quite complete without the nuns, though they had, of course, not appeared in the enactment of the pageant. Without their guidance, without their supervision, its development would have been different and so would its character; therefore, in a sense, they were an integral part of it. They belonged with their charges.

I shall always be glad that, in the end, they felt this way about it too.

I have said a great deal about the Ragus family, but so far there has been one conspicuous omission for which I must make up before I go on to other subjects. I have not told you anything about Coralie's husband, Mr. Ragus.

He is a huge, easy-going, good-natured man, by vocation a truck driver, by avocation a gardener, a plumber, a painter and a jack-of-all-trades. But for him I doubt if the garden would bloom so brightly, for, as I have remarked in passing, Coralie's main interest lies inside, rather than outside the house. Coralie probably prods him on, for he is not a human dynamo like her. But I shall never forget one occasion when he acted on his own initiative.

It was like this: Demon, the Ragus' cocker spaniel, while still young, trusting and innocent, was led astray by a white Spitz. The result of this transgression was a snowy litter, which it would have been hard to characterize as belonging to any particular breed, but which was just as cute as it could be, for all that. Coralie resented it. Demon did not exactly resent it, but she was too young to take the responsibilities of motherhood seriously; or perhaps she tardily recognized her offspring as a badge of shame. At all events, the small white puffballs needed more attention and especially more nourishment than they were getting.

One sunny afternoon when I was having my hair washed, the truck came roaring into the blossoming yard and Mr. Ragus climbed out of it. I could hear his hearty voice and his solid step. Normally, he did not come home at that hour or, indeed, until several hours later. My curiosity was aroused. With my head still dripping, I went to the window of the Parisienne Beauty Salon and looked out.

The pups were comfortably clustered on the well-cut grass and in front of them squatted Mr. Ragus. In his hand he held a large nursing bottle, filled with milk. With practiced impartiality, he fed each of the hungry pups in succession, and each, recognizing the imminence of satisfied repletion, patiently waited his turn. Obviously, this was a regular occurrence. When the nursing bottle was empty, Mr. Ragus put it in his pocket, remounted the seat of his truck, and drove noisily away to resume his normal occupation of delivering laundry.

Since that day I have always liked Mr. Ragus very much.

COFFEE ACROSS CANAL STREET

When I long nostalgically for Richmond, as I often do, it is not only for the place, as a beautiful city, built like Rome on seven hills; it is not even for the people, as friends who have meant much to me all my life. It is also for the strange sweet scent which drifts in all directions from the great tobacco warehouses down by the James River. This scent must be borne on every breeze that blows, for I have often been aware of it before I was otherwise conscious that I was nearing my destination. But, with the first whiff of it, I have known that I was coming home.

In like measure, after I have crossed Canal Street in New Orleans and entered Magazine on my way uptown, it is not primarily the change in the general character of the buildings and the crowds which strikes me; it is the fact that I am approaching the great wholesale establishments which deal in the export and import of various essential commodities; and this fact proclaims itself by the delightful aroma of roasting coffee. I usually find this fragrance a source of irresistible temptation; I decide to postpone the accomplishment of whatever purpose originally brought me to this section of the city, and stop in at the headquarters of J. Aron and Company for rest and refreshment.

This establishment, which is one of the largest importer-distributor concerns in the coffee world, is quartered in a beautiful old corner house, made of rose-colored brick and adorned with double balconies of wrought iron. The elegance of its exterior, which suggests leisurely and luxurious living rather than mercantile operations is, in a sense, deceiving; for within, it is the scene of varied and intensive activities. Directly inside the door is a circular, revolving table, used for "tasting" coffee. In the center of its glistening black surface stands a tall tumbler, filled with scalding water, for the reception and sterilization of tasters' spoons; and around this are ranged . . .

. . . a number of pans, containing different "chops" or lots of coffee, both green and roasted, each ticketed with its shipping mark, record of quantity on hand and name of the steamer by which it has arrived. Encircling these pans, at the very edge of the table, are the white testing cups, bearing the trademark of the company and made of the very thin china which expedites the cooling process and thereby enables the taster to work more quickly. Attached to the base of the table, under the ledge, are two dental basins, which serve the same purpose as the now outmoded cuspidor. For, at this table sits at least one taster—most frequently the veteran, Adam Huhner, who has been at this business for more than thirty years. The taster first dips his spoon into one of the white cups which has been filled with coffee brew; then, making a gargling sound, sucks it back to his palate as a spray; and finally spits it out into the gleaming basin. This "cupping" process enables him to determine the merits or defects of the various coffees he is sampling and to establish their respective values; it is of vital importance to the industry.

Back of the tasting table is the imposing array of modern equipment for the sales department, and still farther to the rear are the private offices of the executives. Midway between the two divisions is a wide doorway leading to . . .

... the coffee bar, where, every afternoon between two-thirty and four, the employees and guests of the company foregather to enjoy their favorite drink in its preferred form, whether this be the "small black," the large *café au lait* or the tall iced glass. Neighboring brokers, bankers and lawyers often drop in to take advantage of this welcome form of entertainment; so do insurance agents, clerks, policemen, postmen, draymen, and representatives of many other tastes and trades. Almost invariably four young secretaries from International House are among the patrons; nearly as regular in their attendance are two members of the clergy. The representatives of these different groups mingle freely and sociably about the bar; then they part to resume the normal occupations which summon them on their several ways.

In the office beyond, the teletype clatters on, the long distance calls keep coming through and secretaries hurry from one desk to another with sheaves of orders to approve, checks to sign and cables to inspect. The pressing business of the day is not, for one moment, dismissed or neglected, since the employees visit the bar in rotation. But the coffee hour eases the tension for everyone and back of it is something more than sound business policy; there is also a spirit of sincere good will and a genius for hospitality. These qualities, equally pronounced in the case of all four presiding executives—two fathers and two sons—together with the harmony which marks their mutual relations, characterize the entire plant as persuasively as the scent of the superb coffee.

The exterior of the building, so typical of the golden age of New Orleans architecture, does not prepare a guest, arriving for the first time, for the ultramodern effect of the ground floor—an effect due not only to equipment and furnishings, but to the striking murals which depict the culture and transportation of coffee. However, if such a guest is fortunate enough to be invited there, he will find the old-time atmosphere scrupulously preserved in the ...

. . . private office where the splendid collection of coffee cups, belonging to "Billy" Burkenroad, one of the vice-presidents, is a prominent feature. These specimens have been assembled from all over the world and the items include cups for *café brûlot* and Turkish coffee; a Royal Doulton R.A.F. cup; a left-handed mustache cup; a large number of intriguing miniatures; and cups with inscriptions which vary all the way from "Coffee Time"—the words surrounding a clock—and "Bet You Can't"—on a cup of mammoth size—to "Present to My Dear Boy" and *"Souffrons les Épines en Espérant les Roses."* ("Let us endure the thorns while hoping for roses.")

The sentiment thus expressed would probably carry more weight elsewhere; it is difficult to concentrate on anything suggestive of an endurance test in so pleasant a place as the private office where "Billy" Burkenroad's collection is installed. And when "Ed" Lafaye, one of the other vice-presidents, acts as host, the privileged guest runs up against another kind of difficulty.

"Ed" does not collect coffee cups as a hobby; instead he collects recipes and, with extraordinary talent, he concocts crab soup, sheepshead salad and various other irresistible dishes. He is one of the best amateur cooks in Louisiana, which is to say, in the world. Even when entertaining at the Lakeshore Club, where the food is justly famous, he invades the kitchen and takes over. The chef is proud to stand aside, recognizing "Ed's" supremacy in the art they both practice. For this is no gilding of refined gold, no painting of the lily; it is a form of creation which bears the unmistakable stamp of genius. He is a big shot at J. Aron and Company and at the Lakeshore Club; but when his attractive daughter, Beverly, became Queen of Hermes, he shone only in reflected glory.

The queens of the major Carnival Balls are chosen months in advance. In this particular instance, the Captain of Hermes had telephoned the invitation to Beverly's parents while they were vacationing in California the preceding September. If a Louisiana parent exists who is not proud to have his daughter so selected, or if a girl has ever paused, even to draw a long breath, before voicing her delighted acceptance, I have yet to hear of it. But "Ed" and Thelma Lafaye actually did wait until their return to New Orleans before "consulting" their daughter. Then a series of conferences was held. The first of these took place at the President's house, where Beverly was shown pictures of former balls and given the necessary details concerning the program of the next one. Until she knew the theme of the tableau, and its color scheme, she could not approach her dressmaker on the subject of a design for her dress; this was the next conference indicated, for the elaborate nature of the royal robes worn at Carnival Balls automatically necessitates lengthy and accomplished workmanship.

CARNIVAL BEGINS ON TWELFTH NIGHT

All Carnival celebrations were suspended during the Second World War, as they have been during previous wars, and, at an unusually early age, she had gone away to college. So she had not experienced the thrill of observing the pageantry of the great balls from the gallery of the Auditorium, where they are held, or of sitting in the "Call-out Section" beneath this balcony, reserved for the guests who are invited to take part in the maskers' dances—privileges which the average society girl accepts as a matter of course from the time she is sixteen. Beverly's excitement over her debut was, therefore, intensified because she attended her first ball—which happened to be Osiris, one of the most spectacular—not as an onlooker or intermittent dancer, but as one of the Queen's Maids. Since Osiris comes much earlier in the schedule of Carnival Balls than Hermes, with numerous others intervening, she— and her parents!—had reason to expect that she might be able to take such festivities a little more in her stride, before her own reign began. However, the very day after her initial appearance . . .

... the automobile in which she was riding skidded on the only ice which had been seen in New Orleans for years, and collided with another car. When the family physician was called in to determine the nature and degree of her injuries, he announced that Beverly had broken two ribs; she could choose between remaining absolutely quiet for a fortnight and jeopardizing her chances of ruling over Hermes!

There could, of course, be but one response to this verdict; but the period of enforced quiet was a severe trial to the patience of the prospective Queen. She was finally released in time to go downtown and see the royal regalia displayed in a show window of Holmes department store—parures consisting of the crowns, sceptres, earrings, necklaces and bracelets to be worn by the Queens of the leading Krewes. Much as a prospective bride steals out of bed for another look at her wedding presents, Beverly gazed at the glittering ornaments destined for the Queen of Hermes. And at last came the great moment . . .

. . . when they were hers to wear.

According to a time-honored custom, the Queen and her entire Court dressed at the home of the Krewe's President; lest this robing process should prove too much of a strain, they were offered refreshments in the form of sandwiches and champagne. Their pictures were taken together and they were escorted to the limousines which were waiting to convey them to City Hall. Then Beverly was suddenly confronted with another difficulty. The plumes which gave the finishing touch to her gorgeous headdress were thirteen inches high; she could not take her appointed place in the limousine without bending over almost double; and, if she did this, she could not lean out of the window, to bow and smile and wave to the populace which had long been foregathered to watch the triumphal progress. There was only one thing to do and it was promptly done: the rear seat of the limousine was detached from its normal place and put on the floor. Beverly sat down on it, adjusting her still unmended ribs to the position as best she could. The motorcade started off with its special police escort. And the Queen, her white plumes waving from the most effective angle, graciously greeted the onlookers along the way.

At City Hall the Mayor and various other dignitaries, together with the previous year's Court of Hermes, were waiting to greet the new Court in the Mayor's parlor —an imposing apartment, elegantly furnished, lined with immense portraits and lighted with crystal chandeliers. A formal address of welcome from His Honor was accompanied by more champagne; then the sound of music heralded the approach of the parade and the arrival of the King, who would toast the Queen from his float. The dignitaries and the Courts hastened outside to take their appointed places on . . .

. . . the reviewing stand, which, fortunately, presented no problems for a high headdress.

Down the street they came—the bands, the torchbearers, the floats, the maskers with their bags from which they tossed all sorts of glittering baubles to the waiting throngs. For the next hour, the procession wound down the long street, filling it with tuneful hilarity and transforming it to a scene of splendor. Then, after the last salute had been given and the last float had passed from view, the Queen and her Maids were once more escorted to their limousines and, again with special police escort, went tearing off to the Court entrance of the Auditorium, where the striped awning overhead and the strip of spotless canvas across the sidewalk alike proclaimed that everything was in readiness for their reception.

According to usual procedure, the Grand March around the Auditorium marks the first triumphal appearance of the Queen there. At this particular ball, there was a slight variation from custom. The tableau represented a reception given by Louis XIV and his Queen to emissaries from all the countries represented in France during the glorious days of the *grand monarque*. Therefore, when the curtain went up, the King and Queen of Hermes were already on their thrones, the "emissaries" were approaching by the palace gates, and the Court of the previous year was ensconced on a balcony. The Grand March—and grand indeed it was—formed the climax and not the prelude to the ceremony.

This Carnival Season ended even more thrillingly than it had begun for Beverly: as current Queen of Hermes, she was entitled, like the Queens of the other major balls, to watch the great Mardi Gras parade . . .

AND ENDS ON MARDI GRAS

... from the front of the Boston Club balcony, where it is reviewed by the Queen of Carnival; and, as a member of the Rex Court, she took an active part in the meeting of Rex and his Queen and Comus and his Queen, with their respective suites, in the presence of their joint Krewes and their chosen guests. This is the supreme moment toward which all celebrations have been converging, ever since the Twelfth Night cake was cut to disclose the golden bean for the Revelers' Queen and the silver beans for her Maids. The girls who, like Beverly (and some ancient Roman whose name I forget) can say, "All of this I saw, part of this I was," never need to say anything else, as far as New Orleans is concerned. However, it is exhilarating to hear a Carnival Queen's impressions from her own lips. And this is how Elizabeth Nicholson, who reigned at Mardi Gras in 1948, described them to Marjorie Roehl of ...

. . . the *New Orleans Item,* which brings out a series of special Carnival issues:

"'It's people cheering you and telling you they like you. It's like when you're small and wake up every few hours on Christmas Eve, wondering if it's morning yet. It's a tremendous thrill, gay and exciting and fun, but it's a little tense too. It's carrying fifty pounds of mantle and crown and sceptre and meeting the Comus Court with every one singing, "If Ever I Cease to Love." It's—well—it's really wonderful.

"'I got up at seven A.M. because I had to be breakfasted and ready by nine A.M. All of us had received innumerable cautions, both oral and in writing, BE PROMPT!' . . .

"The Queen and her Maids appeared on the Boston Club balcony about eleven A.M. and stayed there, waving and smiling, until the parade was over. 'We wanted to stay and watch all the trucks,' Miss Nicholson remembered. 'But as everything had to move on schedule, we went inside and had lunch about two P.M. Then at four I had to rush home and dress for the ball. . . .

" ' . . . To carry your train more easily . . . you're harnessed into a canvas contraption under your dress. Your shoulders, ribs, waist and even your knees are strapped to your train. That is supposed to make your balance easier. I was wearing high heels to make me a little taller and the more I thought of the possibility [of having my heels buckle under all this weight] the worse it seemed. So I had the shoes reinforced with metal. And that was heavy too. But at the time you don't notice the discomfort. Everything is too wonderful, too exciting. And then there's that tremendous climax of the meeting of Rex and Comus. And afterwards you go home, so sorry it's all over. It's only when you take the crown off you realize it was heavy.' "

Locally, the Comus Ball, which takes place on Mardi Gras at the same time as the Rex Ball, is generally considered the most select, though several others are quite as beautiful and many outsiders need to be reminded that all are private functions. The girl who reigns as Queen of Comus, like the girl who reigns as Queen of Rex, is always chosen from the most exclusive social circles and shares many of the latter's honors. In the Grand March, which brings the Balls to an end, Comus and Rex exchange partners; and, at the Queen's Supper which follows the Balls, the King of Carnival proudly takes his places between the two Queens. But when the feast is over and one last toast has been drunk in the inexhaustible champagne, the strains of the Carnival song, "If Ever I Cease to Love," die away in the distance and the gorgeous purple and green and gold flags come down from all the houses where former Queens live. And finally the lights go out.

TO BE FOLLOWED BY THE SPRING FIESTA

For many years, Carnival was the one outstanding festival season in New Orleans. Contrary to the impression which seems to prevail, except in the regions where such celebrations are an integral part of the people's life, Carnival and Mardi Gras are not synonymous. The former begins on Twelfth Night, that is to say, on January sixth and culminates on Shrove Tuesday, or Mardi Gras, the day before Ash Wednesday, which may fall anywhere between the third of February and the ninth of March, depending on the date of Easter; so Mardi Gras represents the culmination of merrymaking and not the entire season devoted to it.

Carnival still represents the zenith of pleasure and pageantry to the average Orleanian; but it is now ushered in by the Sugar Bowl Game, which takes place on New Year's Day and which is the occasion of such widespread and prolonged excitement that Twelfth Night seems more like a continuation of it than a revival of it; and the sackcloth and ashes which signify the beginning of the Lenten Season are swept aside by the billowing skirts of the ladies responsible for the Spring Fiesta.

This celebration, which is sponsored by a non-profit organization called the New Orleans Spring Fiesta Association, was incorporated in 1939 . . .

... "for the purpose of emphasizing the culture and colorful phases of old Louisiana as well as creating interest in the modern Creole state." The Fiesta is produced by many prominent persons and groups "working in unison to make the schedule of events attractive to the visiting public and representative of the best in New Orleans past and present. Private clubrooms and homes, ordinarily closed to visitors, are opened as a courtesy to the Spring Fiesta's guests; and gracious, costumed hostesses welcome the guests at all Fiesta stops."[5]

In the first years of the Association's existence, the number of attractions it offered were limited and its program was confined to a single week. Now the calendar of events has been lengthened to a fortnight for the tours, receptions and art exhibit; and these are later supplemented by the Spring Fiesta Horse Show. The tours include not only downtown and uptown homes in their itineraries, but a Bayou Lafourche Plantation Tour and a St. Tammany Parish Home and Garden Tour. There are separate tours which permit the visitor to view ...

. . . "Courtyards and Crinolines" and "Patios by Candlelight."

The former tour takes place in the daytime and features the small, intimate court-yards. The old families, who built these to insure seclusion, have naturally been reluctant to forego it. It is due largely to the efforts of one of their own clan, Mrs. Jefferson Davis Hardin, Jr., that they have been persuaded to allow outsiders to penetrate to them and to the more spacious and formal patios which are the ones visited by candlelight. They are no lovelier than the others; but they lend them-selves better to evening entertainment, as they offer more room for the performances of the strolling singers who go to each in turn. When the singers have departed, and the sound of their voices dies away in the distance, the dripping fountains still make their own music; and the illusion of a recreated past is more complete after night-fall, especially when the moonlight streams down over the exquisite costumes and flowering shrubs and makes shadowy patterns on the ancient walls and flagstones.

The Spring Fiesta culminates in a pageant called . . .

. . . "A Night in Old New Orleans."

Here the scene is not confined to a single patio or even a succession of these; it embraces a large part of the French Quarter, which is brilliantly and appropriately decorated for the occasion. Modern traffic is barred from the streets and ancient carryalls and coaches take over. Flower vendors and praline women, troubadors and guitar players wander through the streets; and fittingly the celebration reaches its climax amidst the splendors of the Pontalba Buildings.

These structures, which flank Jackson Square on either side, themselves vividly recall the fabulous heiress by whom they were planned and built and whose name they still bear; Michaela Almonaster, daughter of Don Andres Almonaster y Roxas, who married her cousin, Joseph Xavier Selestin Delfan de Pontalba. According to certain stories, she renounced her true love and gave her hand without her heart. Be this as it may, a radiant aura still surrounds her name and the galleries where the initials "A" and "P" are intertwined remain the setting for undying romance.

A SHOTGUN HOUSE IN MID-CITY

The terms "French Quarter" and "Vieux Carré" soon become familiar to every visitor in New Orleans. He learns, if he did not already know it, that the original walled city of the French founders, which lies below Canal Street, was laid out in the form of a square and that either designation is, therefore, appropriate. He also learns that, after the Louisiana Purchase, the Americans who came in built above Canal Street, which formed a dividing line between the section to which the old inhabitants clung and the one which the newcomers frequented. The expansive style of building and landscaping in the uptown development led to its designation as "the Garden District," and he hears this so often that it too is soon familiar.[6] He is seldom so quickly acquainted with the term "Mid-City"; and, as a matter of fact, I think he will really understand the whole layout, which is confusing, to say the least, only after consulting a map. The Crescent City is bordered on one side by Lake Pontchartrain and on the opposite side by the Mississippi River. Halfway between the two is the district now known as "Mid-City."

It is not a particularly fashionable section, but it is a pleasant one. The people who live there seem to be more neighborly, in the small town sense of the word, than in most metropolises. The corner grocer and the druggist just down the street are your friends. Children who live in the same block play games together and housewives call to each other across backyard fences. Nearly all the yards are small, which adds to the ease of communication. The houses are small too, and a large proportion of them are built in the "shotgun" style which is especially characteristic of New Orleans —that is to say, with one room directly behind the other. The term is said to come from the rather gruesome fact that a man standing in the front room of such a house could shoot straight through to the rear and hit a man standing in the back room without impediment—and that not infrequently he did.

Fortunately, there is nothing gruesome about my own affiliations with shotgun houses. I have pleasant associations with several of them. The one to which I go most frequently belongs to my friends Mr. and Mrs. Perry Adams.

There is nothing to distinguish the exterior from hundreds of other shotgun houses, except that it is rather sprucer looking than many, and the arrangement of the five small rooms which form the interior follows the inevitable pattern. But there the run-of-the-mill resemblances end. For both Mr. and Mrs. Adams not only have a passion for antiques, but a comprehensive knowledge of these; through a combination of heirlooms with careful purchases, they have achieved an ensemble of "early Louisiana in detail" which approaches perfection. A "wig dresser" of thuja wood and a Seignouret wine cabinet are only two among many precious items. Every lamp in the house is a museum piece; the collection of Waterford glass is unique. The tiny garden in the rear . . .

... reveals Mrs. Adams' genius for selection and arrangement in the same definite way as the interior. She has used the marble tops of old tables and washstands for stepping stones, disposing them in a symmetrical design. Ships' lanterns form the lighting fixtures. A Parian statuette of Prometheus serves as presiding deity. Petunias and caladium grow in profusion; and ivy veils the walls of the old washhouse which is now Mrs. Adams' studio. For she is more than a collector; she is also a decorator and a restorer; broken china, battered paintings, decrepit furniture all regain their beauty and meaning under her skillful touch.

Among her treasures are some beautiful *veilleuses*,[7] which I have never known anyone else in the United States, except myself, to collect, though doubtless these exquisite items must have other *aficionados*. Recently, on my return from Europe, I brought her a very old and rare *veilleuse* from Carcassonne as a present, parting from it with real regret, for I could easily visualize the proud place it might occupy among my own. This regret was considerably enhanced when Mrs. Adams took a plain white *veilleuse* of the same size and shape, which she had tracked down with characteristic perspicacity, and painted it to ...

. . . match the one I had bought her. I defy anybody but an expert to tell which is the original and which is the copy; and the pair are, of course, twice as effective in the general arrangement of a collection as the single piece would have been!

Among the old paintings which Mrs. Adams has ferreted out and skillfully restored is one of the famous—or infamous—Jean Lafitte—smuggler, corsair, dealer in "black ivory" and intrepid soldier of fortune. Her colored maid, Lucinda, became deeply interested in this restoration and in the identity of the portrait. After a brief outline of Lafitte's prowess, Mrs. Adams defined him as a pirate. Lucinda appeared dissatisfied with this definition, and throughout the rest of the day, her usual calm countenance had a worried look. When she was leaving, somewhat earlier than usual, because her daughter was graduating from a "beauty saloon" and she desired to be present at the celebration, she gave voice to her bewilderment. "Miss Helène," she said, "I wish you tells me why for you calls de gennel'man in de picture a parrot."

Jean Lafitte has been identified in countless ways; but I believe this special designation is original with Lucinda.

ST. JOSEPH'S ALTARS

I enjoy going to the Garden District and to Mid-City, but I am glad that I live in the Vieux Carré; I have grown extremely fond of it. There is a mellowness about its mood as well as its buildings. I relish the wonderful cheeses that I get at Montalbano's and the cassata that I get at Brocato's. I am cheered by the gay snatches of song that come floating into my patio and by the friendly sound of steamboat whistles on the river. I feel privileged to live across the street from the old Ursuline Convent. In fact, I enjoy all the local celebrations. Outstanding among these is the commemoration of St. Joseph's Day.

This feast, falling on March 19, is the occasion for the erection of special, temporary altars in many shops and homes as thank offerings for favors granted. On the framework of the door leading into such a store or dwelling place, branches of fresh bay leaves are fastened, in a manner reminiscent of the sign of the first Passover. Sometimes, there is a printed notice as well; but it is the fresh green sprays which most significantly tell the story.

Within, the largest and most important apartment has been set aside and decorated in a fashion so profuse as to be almost bewildering: first comes a canopy, usually made of a billowing lace overlay on bright silk. Under this a long table is laden with edibles of every conceivable description other than flesh foods. But there is everything else and it has all been prepared, over a period of weeks, lovingly and by hand: brittle bundles of macaroni, flaky mounds of rice, mammoth loaves of bread. Conical green artichokes, luscious red strawberries, golden wine encased by basketry. Shrimp, crabs and crayfish. Chocolate eclairs, mocha layer cakes, brilliant beadlike candy. At the rear, the statue of St. Joseph rises benignly. On either side, decorated candles shed their soft light and fragrant flowers their perfume. At the front, places are laid as for a feast. It is plain that this has been prepared for honored guests.

Let us visit one of these altars early in the morning, when the parish priest goes to bless it; we will find these honored guests among our fellow visitors. They are children of the family or of the neighborhood, and they tell us gravely but proudly that they are "saints." Our first reaction to this announcement is apt to be one of startled surprise, for it must be confessed that there is nothing especially holy about the appearance of most of the small urchins, who come crowding around. But our cue is to ask, "Which saint are you?" and the way the child answers shows that for that day at least he is trying to assume the attributes of a holy man. He has not failed to confess the night before and communicate that morning, now he is to eat at the "Saints' Table." He must be worthy of this honor. For sometimes even the Blessed Mother and the Christ Child Himself are represented at the feast.

85

SHREVEPORT

HAS HAD A LUSTY HISTORY

Shreveport, the city second to New Orleans in size, has had a lusty history. It was named for Henry Miller Shreve, a trader and steamboat builder, to whom the United States Government had assigned the task of opening the Red River for navigation. He was without doubt what is generally known as a colorful character and he had an equally colorful career, in which floating battering rams, nitroglycerine and Caddo Indians all added to the gaudy decor. But he got results. He began his work on Red River in 1833 and, within a year, it was free for a distance of eighty miles of the log jam which had blocked it. After that, progress was steady. Shreveport was incorporated in 1839 and "the development of trade had been well begun before the town itself was organized. Business came with every hunter and every trapper that brought packs of peltries out of the wilderness; it came with every covered wagon that rolled its way westward; with every flat boat, barge and steamboat that pushed its way through the channel that Shreve and his floating battering rams had opened. . . . Flush times came to Shreveport . . . money was plentiful and life was gracious and gay. . . . Every boat . . . was loaded . . . with bales of cotton. . . . With the discovery of oil in 1906 in Caddo Lake . . . Shreveport began to boom in earnest. Today oil is the dominant feature in Shreveport's economic life."[8]

To me this word picture is one of the most vivid which can be traced to the genius of Lyle Saxon; but I hope that some day this, and other glowing accounts, will be supplemented by a great historical novel with Henry Miller Shreve as its hero and Shreveport as its setting. Meanwhile, scenes depicting the city's progress have been created through the unusual medium of dioramas, housed in the Louisiana State Exhibit Building. Its curator, H. B. Wright, is recognized as one of the leading dioramists in the world, and he has done a magnificent piece of work, which is finely displayed.

86

—WHICH IS CLEVERLY INTERPRETED
THROUGH DIORAMAS

The response to this exhibit is enormous, but it is almost disconcertingly observant; therefore every individual item must be flawless. And it is. One visitor, scrutinizing a diorama which showed a loading platform on a railroad siding, inquired why the clothing of the workers was so spotless. "Because," Mr. Wright replied instantly, "they have just arrived for the day. It is very early in the morning. If you will look a little more closely, you will see that the mist of pre-dawn still covers the landscape." And so it does!

Normally, all the materials which Mr. Wright needs are supplied by the museum. But occasionally a long search for something he greatly needs ends at his own fireside. One day his wife came home wearing with pride a hat which she had just purchased. Mr. Wright fixed his eyes upon it and Mrs. Wright steeled herself for the usual kind of husbandly remark about headgear. "That veil looks exactly like chicken wire!" Mr. Wright exclaimed. But his tone was not one of criticism; it was one of triumph. He had long been searching to secure the wherewithal to supply the last necessary detail in a diorama depicting Louisiana's poultry industry!

AND SPECIALIZES
IN MODERN INDUSTRIAL ARCHITECTURE

Shreveport has its own prototype for the French Market of New Orleans. This is the Big Chain, which now has branches all over the city, though it began in a modest way: near the turn of the century a small grocery store known as Wiener-Loeb was managed by a youngster named Ed Wile. Together with two other youngsters —D. R. Sandefur, who had just graduated from the Minden High School, and Louis Levy, who was running a produce store—he took over Wiener-Loeb.

The industry, ability and perseverance of these three made possible the present Big Chain, that consists of six fine stores. Outstanding among these, from the viewpoint of modern architecture, is the huge Broadmoor establishment. This is by no means the only example of modern industrial architecture of which Shreveport is justly proud. It has many and among these—believe it or not—is the city incinerator. This has been selected by experts as one of the twenty-five best buildings east of the Rockies and models of it have been chosen for display at the San Francisco Exhibition, in the New York Museum of Modern Art and in the United States Pavilion at the Paris International Exhibition. The Architectural Forum has pronounced it the "first major United States building of its kind where complete design and . . .

... supervision service have been rendered by a firm of architects." (Jones, Roessle, Olsehner and Wiener.) Many stories are told about it, including one concerning Mr. William Lescaze, an eminent New York architect and lecturer. According to this story, Mr. Lescaze wrote to Mr. Wiener, after seeing a picture of the incinerator, and asked what material had been used in the coping. It appeared to be stainless steel; but if it were, wasn't that a mighty rich material for such a purpose? Mr. Wiener replied, "It is indeed stainless steel and that is indeed a mighty rich material. But perhaps you do not realize that through this building passes the garbage of our best families."

Certain residential sections of Shreveport are very beautiful. The city's wealth reveals itself in large handsome houses, surrounded by spacious grounds and gardens, magnificently maintained. The Richard W. Norton Art Foundation, at present under development, will provide Shreveport with one of the finest art centers in the country for a place of its size. Cross Lake, a few miles distant, which supplies the city with water, also affords ample sport in the form of boating and fishing. The statement that "money was plentiful and life gracious and gay" does not apply only to Shreveport's early boom times. It applies equally well to the present.

89

I WOULD BE PROUD TO MOUNT
THE DAVIS BAND WAGON

One of the loveliest ladies I have had the good fortune to meet since coming to Louisiana is Mrs. Jimmie Davis of Shreveport, whose husband was governor of the State while I was living in the Cottage on the River Road near Baton Rouge. She was a schoolteacher in her youth, but there is nothing to suggest the traditionally stiff schoolmarm in her manner, which is quiet, gracious and warm. She is sincerely religious and grace is an established rule at her table, even at formal functions.

The Davises are extremely cordial by nature and their natural inclination toward hospitality was facilitated during Mr. Davis' encumbency by an excellent housekeeper and an experienced household staff. Louisiana provides its governors with a commodious mansion and, besides a suitable salary, gives them an ample allowance for entertaining and contingent expenses. Governors—not to mention governors' wives!—who have had to provide their own living quarters and to run these on salaries as small as $3,000 a year, are well qualified to estimate the singularly great blessings that Louisiana bestows upon its chief executive in regard to finances.

Louisiana also takes it for granted that its governors will not devote all their time to affairs of state, but spend a certain amount of it in whatever form of relaxation is agreeable to them. Jimmie Davis is an expert angler and enjoys getting away on a fishing trip. But—next to his wife, of course—music is his real love. He has composed tuneful airs for any number of ditties, of which *You Are My Sunshine* is probably the best known; and he delights in rendering these himself with his famous hillbilly band, sometimes called the "Sunshine Band" after the song. He has had a tremendous success in Hollywood and he carried his movie methods into his campaigning, where they were equally successful. I am not surprised. He continued to conduct his band all the time he was governor and I have listened to it a number of times with great enjoyment.

While they were in the Mansion the Davises, who are childless, adopted a baby whom they nicknamed "Skipper" and in whom the whole State has taken a lively interest. He is a delightful little boy and the feeling is natural. So is the interest the Davises themselves continue to arouse. They are an engaging couple and their home town is justly proud of them.

BATON ROUGE

THE OLD CAPITOL AND—

As the visitor approaches Baton Rouge, he is confronted with large billboards announcing that he will soon have the privilege of seeing "the most beautiful capitol in America." I am inclined to disagree. I think Bulfinch did fairly well with the capitol in Boston and Thomas Jefferson with the one in Richmond. But even if there were no such standards of comparison, the immensely high tower of the capitol in Baton Rouge seems to me out of harmony with the level landscape of Louisiana, and the interior is showy and spacious, rather than stately. Personally, the Old Capitol, which now houses various minor government offices, interests me more.

I say this stoutly, though Mark Twain derided it "as a little sham castle," and I myself feel that the classic ante-bellum style would have been a more logical choice than the pseudomedieval. But somehow the "little sham castle" seems appropriate for its setting; and its interior has elements of real beauty.

THE OLD AND NEW UNIVERSITY

I feel something the same way about the old and new university buildings that I do about the old and new capitols. The old university buildings, generally called the Pentagon, are, in my opinion, the most beautiful in Baton Rouge and among the most beautiful in Louisiana. There are four of these, almost identical, which inclose an open area with the river on the fifth side, thus forming a pentagon. Their long galleries are supported by Doric columns which run their full length, both front and back; the gateways which lead to their inclosure have dignity and grace; and the surrounding trees are magnificent.

The new university buildings were erected during the nineteen-twenties and their style is designated both as "domestic Italian" and "California colonial." Again, it seems to me a pity that the classic ante-bellum type of architecture, which so definitely belongs to Louisiana, was not chosen. But the plant is a fine one, providing up-to-date educational facilities for about ten thousand students. The black iron kettle, in which Etienne de Bore boiled the first sugar-cane juice to be granulated in Louisiana, is one of the sights of the University; so is Mike the tiger, the mascot of the football team, whose immense cage occupies an equally prominent position.

The evidences of modern progress, in which Baton Rouge abounds, seem to me the most arresting sights in the Capital City. For instance . . .

93

THE NEW RUBBER

... "cold" rubber.

This substance, according to official reports, is made from "Butadiene and Styrene, both petroleum products." This definition will probably be as baffling to the average amateur as it is to me. Even the information that the "basic ingredients are oil and coal, along with such simple additions as sugar, soap, salt, phosphate and acid" does not help much; or the additional statement to the effect that "the refrigeration is highly important because cold rubber is processed at forty-one degrees." But we can all grasp, without difficulty and with considerable awe, the following statements as to the consequences of the process which results in cold rubber:

It makes tires wear thirty per cent longer.

It can make the United States independent of natural rubber.

Cold rubber was first produced on a commercial scale in February, 1948, at the Copolymer Corporation in Baton Rouge. By May of 1949 the plant was turning out nothing else and was producing 33,000 tons a year.

Elemore Morgan, who saw the processing of the first cold rubber tire, describes it this way:

"The total time involved was less than three minutes. The operator pulled a wide sheet of raw material from the stock shelves near his machine and drew it across a revolving drum. After two such sheets had been rolled around the drum, he placed the 'beads' (i.e., four strips of wire wrapped in rubber) on the edges of the tire 'carcass,' and then put two more pieces of raw material on top of those. Automatic stitchers, with which the machine was supplied, pressed the raw material together until it formed a laminated mass. Next, the breaker strip was applied to the carcass and the tread was added to it. Finally the drum was collapsed and the tire, ready for vulcanizing, was withdrawn."

94

The realization of what this process would mean to the traveling public was, naturally, almost overwhelming to a sensitive and appreciative onlooker; but the new tire represents an important step forward, not an initial experiment, in the production of synthetic rubber. It is perhaps even more moving to realize that a score of men, working together since the early part of World War II, in one small Louisiana factory, have been able to turn out as much material, in any given time, as all the thousands toiling in the rubber-producing areas of the Amazon Valley and the East Indies.

The vats, filled with creamy, foaming liquid, the pebble-like granulations tumbling from steel conveyors, the great sheets of substance flowing from the mills ready for cutting and distribution—all these make a thrilling sight. But the consciousness of its significance is even more stirring than the spectacle itself.

The experiments with synthetic rubber, which have had such far-reaching results, have been made by the Louisiana Division of . . .

STRANGE BEAUTY—THE STANDARD OIL PLANT

... the Esso Standard Oil Company of New Jersey.

Its immense plant covers almost three square miles and employs eight thousand persons. While still miles from Baton Rouge, the approaching traveler sees its great "cat-crackers" towering above the landscape; and at night, when these are lighted, they are curiously suggestive of a New York skyline in miniature. The flares, with their billowing flames, add to the radiance of the scene. But they are not merely ornamental; they serve as safety valves for dangerous gases. The Horton spheres, gleaming with white paint, form still another arresting feature of the refinery; and they too perform an important function as storage tanks for gases kept under high pressure.

During World War II, the major part of all the octane gasoline used for military aviation, not only for ourselves but for our allies, came from this Baton Rouge plant; so did the fire bombs extensively used against the Japanese. In peacetime, its output is almost as impressive and even more comprehensive. There is hardly a commodity in general use throughout the world whose manufacture is not either directly or indirectly connected with some of the products of this refinery, which number seven hundred. The average person instinctively thinks of gasoline, kerosene, lubricants, asphalt and fuel oil in connection with it; much rarer is the realization that wax, wood preservatives, insecticides, pharmaceutical supplies and cosmetics come from there too. Its Research Department has produced results which have affected the oil industry everywhere; its Personnel Department has developed a system of pensions, hospitalization and other benefits which is considered a model in the field of industrial welfare. Fifteen per cent of the employees live on farms, working forty hours a week at the plant and giving the rest of the time to their private pursuits; many others, retiring while they are still in the prime of life, do not work at all, but devote their unlimited leisure to fishing and other congenial diversions.

I have heard several stories along these lines; the one which has always appealed to me most, concerns a Negro who found himself short of cash, after being at the plant some six or seven years. Going to the Annuities and Benefits window, he inquired whether it would be possible for him to secure a hundred-dollar loan. "Certainly," the cashier replied, "but you have about fifteen hundred dollars to your credit already." ... "Ah *is?*" inquired the startled beneficiary of the industry's wise planning. "Kin Ah have it?" ... "Certainly," the cashier replied a second time. "Whenever you wish." ... "Ah'll come back an' get it nex' week," the Negro said conclusively. "Ah kin fix to retire by then. Ain't no use one rich man workin' for another."

Which is a remarkably sound piece of philosophy.

STARK GENIUS—THE SACRED HEART CHURCH

On the outskirts of Baton Rouge, going toward New Orleans, are three interesting burying grounds: the National Cemetery, which contains the graves of nearly two thousand United States soldiers; the Magnolia Cemetery, which "was the scene of the fiercest fighting in the Battle of Baton Rouge"; and the old Catholic Cemetery, where the tombs display a degree of originality rare even in Louisiana, one of them being surmounted by a dollhouse!

Just beyond these ancient, well-shaded cemeteries, the yellow-brick pile of the new Sacred Heart Church rises in bold relief against the sky. It is architecturally effective, ·but it is not yet mellowed by time and its outlines are still unsoftened by trees. However, the visitor who has found its exterior arresting rather than attractive had better take a deep breath before stepping inside; for its walls are decorated with some of the most startling frescoes that have been painted since the days of Cimabue.

These murals are the work of a Belgian Benedictine by the name of Gregory de Witt. The Abbot of St. Meinrad, while visiting at Louvain, was struck by Father Gregory's extraordinary talents and invited him to Indiana. After his arrival there, the young Belgian made the acquaintance of Monsignor Blasco of Baton Rouge, who, in turn, besought him to decorate the new Sacred Heart Church in the capital of Louisiana. Monsignor Blasco was deeply gratified when Father de Witt undertook the commission; but if any other works of art have, in late years, been the subject of so much local controversy, I do not know of it.

Above the altar looms a gigantic painting of Christ, inspired by the famous mosaic at Palermo and strikingly reminiscent of it. Facing each other, on either side of the nave, are interpretations of the woman of Samaria and the Magdalene, done in brilliant colors and bold design. But the fourteen paintings which mark the Stations of the Cross are, I believe, the most overwhelming of all. Having glanced at them briefly, the amazed beholder may turn away, intending to look no more. But, almost inevitably, he will find himself looking at them again and the second look will be longer. Whether this attention is voluntary or not, the paintings compel it.

All but the first and last stations are in the nave; these two are placed in the transept. If they were less remarkable, they might easily be overlooked by the average sightseer. As it is, their very remoteness acts as a challenge. I shall never know how long I stood, spellbound, before the representation of the dead Christ. For the first time in my life I clearly envisaged the tomb belonging to Joseph of Arimathaea, which he had hewn out of the rock, and the clean linen cloth in which he had wrapped the body, and Mary Magdalene and the other Mary, "sitting over against the sepulcher."

CLINTON

LAWYERS' ROW

Baton Rouge is, essentially, a modern city. Its most rapid growth has all taken place in recent years and the Pentagon Building is almost its only remaining example of Greek Revival architecture. Its major activities also belong to the present and it pursues them with more bustle than is the habit of most places in the Deep South. On the other hand, Clinton, the parish seat of East Feliciana, retains much the same aspect and atmosphere that it did more than a century ago and its people unconcernedly follow their leisurely pursuits. But, like those extolled by Solomon, its paths are paths of pleasantness and all its ways are peace.

Probably its most famous feature is the so-called Lawyers' Row, a group of five small, columned buildings, built in the eighteen-twenties. They were first occupied by twelve Clinton barristers, whose standards were so high that lawyers came from all parts of the State to confer with them. Only one of the beautiful little buildings is still occupied by a lawyer, but he is a descendant of the original owner.

100

OLD COURTHOUSE

Opposite Lawyers' Row is the old courthouse. Even in midafternoon, its colonnade is apt to be practically deserted. An old colored man, the only person then in sight, once stopped Elemore Morgan and inquired whether he took pictures of people for pay; he was getting on in years, the man said, and would like to have a photograph of himself. Elemore was naturally glad to accommodate him as a matter of courtesy, and eventually asked him what was bringing him to the courthouse. He replied that he had come to clear up a tax question. It then transpired that he was the owner of some three hundred acres. Half of this land had been given his mother by her white folks when they freed her; the rest he had acquired himself. He had two tenants on it. But he did not depend on them for his entire revenue. He was a chimney builder[9] and carpenter by trade. Obviously he had prospered.

He gave Elemore his name and address and shuffled quietly away. The silence of complete emptiness again pervaded the beautiful colonnade.

PLAQUEMINE

ROUSTABOUTS ON THE LEVEE

Plaquemine is a small city on the west bank of the Mississippi, about twenty-five miles north of Donaldsonville. Between the two, sugar cane grows abundantly and there are numerous fine plantations, where the prodigality of the past blends pleasantly and profitably with the progress of the present. It was in this locality that the mysteries of carriers and crushers, filter presses and juice pumps, centrifugals and feeder rakes, were first revealed to me; and I shall not soon forget the roasted doves which formed part of a Thanksgiving feast at Catherine, the sugar house party at Cora Texas or the picnic lunch in the garden of St. Louis, where the "green" rose, which was the marvel of the countryside a century ago, still enthralls the privileged beholder.

Yes, Plaquemine is certainly fortunate in its location, for there is no end to the interesting things that can be seen and done in its immediate vicinity and I have not so much as hinted at half of them. Furthermore, it is the proud possessor of vast steel locks, where the "lift" is said to be the highest in the world, and oil and lumber, as well as sugar, have added to its prosperity.

Formerly all this produce was shipped by barge via Bayou Plaquemine; now tank cars are gradually supplanting the barges. But the barrels of molasses, stacked in great tiers beside the bayou near the little bridge at the north end of town, were a great sight in their day, and I have often stopped to look at them in the course of my wanderings. At night, after the roustabouts had left the levee bank, the scene gave the impression of tranquil abundance; in the daytime, when the men were working, the sound of their shouting and swearing rang out above the sound of creaking chains and rolling weight.

102

Plaquemine has boasted a surprising number of millionaires for a place of its size. But it has few outstanding architectural attractions and Meriam is an inconspicuous street, lined on either side with unpretentious houses. The one where the Trosclairs live is made of stucco, and, in spite of the high steps leading up to it, is rather flat of appearance. The front rooms are tidy and comfortable, but they are more or less stereotyped. You get the feeling that they are there more because it is customary for all civilized persons to have such rooms than because they mean a great deal to the Trosclair family. However, when you reach the kitchen . . .

A CATERESS AND HER CAKES

. . . you feel there never was such a kitchen—at least that is the way I felt, though many a one before this has moved me to envious admiration. But Mrs. Trosclair's is different. Not only because it is spotless and sunnier than most; not only because it has more white tiling, a better refrigerator and a bigger deep freeze than most; not even because its gas range has more gadgets for regulating heat and turning lights and burners on and off and generally facilitating cookery than half a dozen ordinary ranges. But because it seems to *matter* so much more than most kitchens, because *this* is the room that seems to count, as far as the Trosclairs are concerned.

I have always maintained that if no one really lived in a room, if it were not constantly used as the center for work and play and companionship, it could never be really homelike or really beautiful either, even if it were in a house inhabited for generations, and even if the most distinguished interior decorator available had planned and arranged it. Mrs. Trosclair's kitchen is homelike and it is beautiful too; and this is largely because she spends so much time in it, and because she shares it with her friends—both the friends who can come to it and enjoy it with her in person and the friends she reaches through her consummate art of cake-making.

At the beginning of the process, this cake-making does not look very different from that of hundreds of other women. But when she has taken an angel food cake from the oven, which is electrically lighted and with a glass door, and set the delicately browned cone out to cool, the difference begins.

Into the hole of the cake goes a small tin can which supports a figurine for which the cake quickly becomes the foundation for a hoopskirt. With this much as the invariable base of operations, the scheme of decoration takes a variety of forms. Usually the figurine is a belle of the sixties, her voluminous skirt either blue or pink, her bodice, bouquet and tip-tilted hat a matching color. But, if the cake is required for a Halloween party, the demure little lady is transformed into a wicked witch, complete with broomstick and tall black hat. If a wedding is imminent, she becomes a bride, her lace veil attached to her hair with tiny spun-sugar gardenias, her spun-sugar bouquet encircled with lace. And, with the approach of Mardi Gras, she enjoys her greatest triumph; then she is a Carnival Queen, with a glittering crown on her head and a long velvet train spread out behind her!

Two of Mrs. Trosclair's daughters are nuns, but there are vocations in the world as well as in the cloister, and I am sure that they feel their mother has one too. At any rate, I have felt that way about it from the first moment that I saw her handiwork. Since I have seen her kitchen, I have been still surer that I was right.

LAFAYETTE

ST. THERESA IS AT HOME HERE

Of all the cities in Louisiana with which I am familiar, Lafayette seems to me the most essentially French, in atmosphere, in viewpoint, in speech and in habit. Therefore, it is fitting that the statue of a French saint—Thérèse de l'Enfant Jésus—should occupy a position of importance and honor, sheltered by the Cathedral Oak, on one of the principal streets.

It seems to belong there. I have never found a region so remote—not the most northern city of the world nor the southernmost—where it appeared out of place; the little saint's appeal is universal, as is the acclaim that has been given her. But, just as there is a difference between a gracious guest and a serene chatelaine, so there is a difference between St. Theresa enshrined in Magallanes and St. Theresa enshrined in Lafayette.

Here she is abundantly surrounded with the things she loved in life and with the things which she promised her faithful followers should be bestowed upon them after her death. As a young nun in Lisieux, already approaching the Valley of the Shadow, she grieved because the trees in the Avenue of Chestnuts, for which she had a special attachment, had been pruned with the unsparing severity of the French and that their branches, already covered with fresh buds, lay withering on the ground. In Lafayette, her statue is surrounded with trees whose luxuriance grows unchecked. "You will not be unhappy after I am gone; I will send a rain of roses to comfort you," she promised on her deathbed. In Lafayette, the flowers that grow at her feet are worthy of her pledge. Only a few blocks away is the Carmelite Convent, governed by the same strict rules, strong in the same power of prayer, as the Carmel of Lisieux which she entered at the age of fifteen and left—for Heaven—nine short years later.

Yes, Lafayette seems a fitting shrine for her. It is a city where Catholicity takes radiant forms and where the beauty of bloom is found on every side. Not only roses are there, but many other lovely flowers—lilies and camellias of every sort, magnolias and azaleas. Lafayette has an Azalea Trail which is rapidly rivaling Mobile's in splendor. It started thirty-three years ago in "a little way." (St. Theresa had a little way too, you will remember.) Miss Anna Bernard, a lady living on Dunreith Street, bought a formosa azalea for twenty-five cents and . . .

THE AZALEA TRAIL STARTED IN A LITTLE WAY

. . . planted it in her garden. A little later, a neighbor, Mrs. Paul Mouton, bought a similar one. This grew and flourished to such a degree that it brought an extravagant compliment from a stranger passing in his buggy. Miss Bernard, Mrs. Mouton and a third neighbor, Mrs. John Montgomery, put their heads together and "vowed to plant more formosas all over the neutral ground. Every time a newcomer moved to their street they gave him layers of formosa and explained their reason for wanting him to set these out in front of his home. Because these three ladies never failed to encourage the beautification of Dunreith, the street has become a reality that is often called the Million Dollar Street of the city."[10]

Another Mouton, generally and affectionately known as "Captain Bob," whose career has been distinguished, both in the Marine Corps and in Congress, is likewise a horticulturist, and, while serving as Mayor of Lafayette, supplied the impetus and the experience for general beautification of the city with shrubs and flowers. The grounds of Southwestern Louisiana Institute present still another example of fine landscaping. Most of this conforms to the more or less standardized manner of planting; but, in addition to the well-massed . . .

A CYPRESS SWAMP ON A CITY CAMPUS

... azaleas and orderly rows of camellias, a natural cypress swamp has been preserved in the center of the campus. Its trees are moss-draped and its banks are lined with iris; its still waters are bright and black as onyx; even on the hottest days the place is cool and shadowy. As the traveler approaches it, his sense of refreshment is mingled with a sense of wonder; he finds it hard to believe that he is still in the heart of a city, surrounded on every side by vigorous and active youth. It seems, instead, as if he had strayed, with almost uncanny swiftness, into the depths of the swamp country.

NATCHITOCHES

A SPIRAL STAIRCASE AND A BRIDAL MEDALLION

Natchitoches is the oldest settlement in the entire area embraced by the Louisiana Purchase; and it has a fabulous history, a great tradition and any number of picturesque reminders of the past. Let a citizen of New Orleans proclaim, in the hearing of a citizen of Natchitoches, that the former city is the most interesting one in the world, and his listener will fairly bristle with indignation.

As the traveler approaches Natchitoches, on a bridge over Red River, a high ruddy bluff, topped with a profusion of pine, looms up before him; the reflection of this in the smooth water is an extraordinary sight, for the Red River is appropriately named and the color contrasts are remarkable. You are still four miles from town when you have crossed the bridge, and you wind along through a pleasant growth of pine until you reach Cane River Lake, one of the finest fishing streams in the state. You have then reached Natchitoches itself.

It is perhaps even more impressive as an entity than in any other way. Many of the old buildings, both public and private, are still standing and the newer ones have taken their tone from these. The result is harmonious, restful and well ordered.

A century or more ago, Natchitoches was an inland port of great consequence; it was the head of river navigation and the point of departure for pioneers pushing farther west. The first experiments of growing cotton on a large scale in Louisiana were made by the sons of Jean Baptiste Prudhomme, more generally known as "Docteur du Roi," who settled in Natchitoches about the middle of the eighteenth century on a land grant obtained from Louis XV; he gave his property the charming name of "Côte Joyeuse" and led a useful as well as a happy life there. Cotton is still the chief product of the region.

The rush of modern progress has bypassed Natchitoches, but it retains much of its ancient magic and its old buildings are rich in romance. Another Prudhomme, Gabrielle, who was an architect, assembled, in Europe, all the materials for his residence and brought them home on a specially chartered vessel; two spiral staircases of "iron lace" were among the features of his splendid establishment. The Tauzin house has hand-hewn cypress sills and rafters and one of the sills conceals a secret chamber. The walls are made of adobe mixed with deer hair. (Allegedly, the builder of the house was a tanner and shipper of deerskins.) "Dowry" houses were common in Natchitoches and one of these has a circular medallion, modeled by an Italian sculptor, in the parlor ceiling; many brides have been married under it since the one for whose delight it was molded.

Besides the famous places in the city proper, there are a number of fine houses in the adjacent country side which form part of the Natchitoches tradition. Probably the best known of these is . . .

MELROSE—EVIDENCE OF ENDURANCE AND GROWTH

. . . Melrose, where the development of plantation architecture can be more effectively observed than almost anywhere else. The first brick house on the place was a simple two-room structure, with a roof projecting far beyond its walls; the African influence of the slaves who built it, and whose sturdy log cabins are still standing behind it, is plainly visible. The second house is much more commodious and shows the beginnings of a different trend; its roof is a far less prominent feature and is supported by cypress posts; galleries at both front and rear supply protection and serve in lieu of corridors, for the rooms lead straight into each other. The third house is . . .

. . . a two-and-a-half-story structure, the roof supported by wooden columns, the gallery by brick pillars; the whole is flanked by hexagonal wings of still later construction and numbers among its various apartments a well-stocked library and an ample dining room.

Of recent years, Melrose has been famous for the personalities which have dominated it, even more than for its architectural importance. Its late chatelaine, Mrs. Cammie Garrett Henry, was known and loved throughout the State; her hospitality was a byword and she was a practical patroness of arts and letters. Lyle Saxon, one of the foremost authors Louisiana has produced, spent months on end as the Henrys' guest and did much of his work there; and he was only one of numerous such beneficiaries. Unlike many other great houses, this one is not dependent on bygone grandeur for its renown.

LAKE CHARLES

"THAT'S WHERE THE WEST BEGINS"

We have already observed the great contrast between Baton Rouge and Clinton; the contrast between Natchitoches and Lake Charles is equally striking. Natchitoches is essentially a city of the Deep South, with all its charming and leisurely characteristics; Lake Charles is almost Western in its atmosphere, energy and enthusiasm. Natchitoches still stresses the glories of the past; Lake Charles envisions a glorious future and rushes forth to grasp at every opportunity which may make this real.

The first settlers were cattlemen. There was plenty of land where stock could graze and the New Orleans market was not too inaccessible, from the very beginning, because of the waterways. It had no white-pillared mansions, surrounded by fields of sugar cane; instead it had ranches and rice farms and lumber mills. A panorama representing its early history would show a broad expanse of sky and prairie; wild flowers and half-wild cattle and horses; fleets of schooners crossing the lake which gave the city its name, laden with lumber for Texas and Mexico; slave traders dealing in human beings at a dollar a pound; cowboys swimming cattle across the Calcasieu River at the rate of two thousand a day and whooping on the great herds lumbering down the Old Spanish Trail; women living in log cabins but wearing silk dresses and fine jewelry on special occasions. . . .

Now a great meat-packing plant and a great chemical plant would loom large in the picture. So would any number of other flourishing industries. In the early nineteen-twenties, the lumber mills had reached the limits of their timber reserves; but the same decade saw the discovery of oil on an old mill site and the beginning of Lake Charles' development as a deep-water seaport. By '48 there were forty-three producing oil and gas wells in and around Lake Charles and it had become the leading seaport in the export of rice. The number of vessels the docks can handle simultaneously is still limited; sometimes flour destined for relief use must be stored in the warehouses to await shipment; but meanwhile cargoes go all over the world. A freighter, loaded with rough rice, should be a welcome sight when it steams into its home port of London.

Average Net August
Paid Circulation
3661
Member Audit
Bureau of Circulation

DAILY ⊕ WORLD

Every day is pay day
for those who
use Want Ads

YOUR FAVORITE NEWSPAPER — MORE NEWS — MORE ADVERTISING — MORE PAID SUBSCRIBERS

Volume IX   Opelousas, Louisiana, Tuesday, October 5, 1948   Number 201

YAMBILEE STAGE SET

Who's King? – Mr. Yam?

Bustling with activity, Louisiana's Yamland is today putting the finishing touches to the third annual Louisiana Yambilee, national sweet potato frolic, and will be host here at Opelousas to thousands of celebrants tomorrow and Thursday.

OPELOUSAS

HOW THE LOCAL PAPER PRINTS ITS NEWS— THE YAMBILEE

Opelousas, which was briefly the capital of Louisiana during the War Between the States, has many of the same characteristics as Lafayette: the French influence still predominates, the pleasures of the table come in for their full share of attention[11] and unpretentious houses are rendered attractive by their setting amidst wide lawns and flowering shrubs. But while the big event of the year in Lafayette is still the Mardi Gras celebration, the "Yambilee" has stolen the limelight in Opelousas.

Locally, the account of this Yambilee is read in *The Daily World*, the first daily newspaper in the United States to be printed by the offset process. The venture has proved so successful that it has now been copied elsewhere; and Rigby Owen, the president and publisher of the paper, was a featured speaker at the New York City convention of the American Newspaper Publishers' Association, where he spoke on the adaptability of his experiment to small-town news sheets. His company has built and is occupying its own plant and is sticking to offset.

Mr. John R. Thistlewaite, editor and vice-president of the paper, tells the story of the Yambilee in his own way, which is a good one. But I have to tell it more briefly in my way, which is like this:

The festival marks the end of the yam or sweet potato harvest, with the arrival of "King Yam" as the opening feature. He comes into town riding on top of a boxcar loaded with sweet potatoes and set upon a float, his face and the upper part of his figure covered with brown papier-mâché to suggest the form and texture of a sweet potato skin. At the courthouse he is presented with the keys to the city and given a bodyguard of "Yamettes," selected among the contestants for Queen. He next reviews a parade of beautiful floats, representing all phases of sweet potato culture; and at the same time another parade takes place, staged by the colored yam growers and preceded by a snappily dressed band from Southern University. Then the King and his Court repair to the park for a program of speeches. A ball, at which a Queen is chosen and crowned, brings the day's activities to an end.

But no festival is permitted to delay the progress of experimentation in the improvement of the sweet potato plant, which goes steadily forward in the laboratory of Dr. Julian C. Miller, head of Horticultural Research at Louisiana State University. Early and late, in and out of season, this brilliant and devoted scientist labors to benefit the product in whose development he has won world fame.

Dr. Miller is the only person who has ever induced sweet potatoes to bloom and come to seed in this climate. This has made possible all the work of breeding new and commercially valuable varieties, most of which has gone on under his direct supervision. He has produced new varieties of strawberries, and is the originator of a process of extracting a new and very fine vegetable oil from okra seeds. But no fanfare is necessary to proclaim his achievements; they have spoken for themselves.

117

HIGHWAYS AND BYWAYS

HIGHWAYS AND BYWAYS

THE WHICHAWAY BUG

THE HAPPY wanderer, starting out on a pleasure journey, naturally makes the question of his route a major concern. In Louisiana, his only difficulty will be in the matter of choice, even if he has a "whichaway bug" to help him!

This is a small insect,[12] which children take between their fingers, tail pointing up, and squeeze lightly as they ask, "Whichaway we go to find Marcel? Whichaway we go to get crayfish? Whichaway the best dewberries?" The bug revolves the tip of its tail and points one way or another. The child trustfully follows directions.

If we can find a whichaway bug, we might pursue something the same method. But if we cannot, it really does not make much difference because all over the state, there are countless beautiful stretches of road, shaded by live oak trees. The trunks and limbs of these oaks are mighty and the leaves are glossy and green all the year round. But the sturdiness and the brightness are veiled by draperies of misty gray moss. Some people say this moss is eerie, others that it is dreary. I do not agree with these opinions. Did you ever see a woman whom a veil did not become? Well, it is the same with a tree!

EVERYWHERE THERE ARE SLEEPY LITTLE
SETTLEMENTS

All over the state, there are also sleepy little settlements, fringing the road and merging into it. Most of the buildings in these settlements are nondescript in themselves; the textures and tints of the woods with which they are built blend, to an extraordinary degree, with the texture and tints of the hanging moss. And neither the lounger on the front porch nor the loafer on the post office steps does anything to dominate the scene; the detached quietude, the hazy warmth have engulfed him too. And, in some cases, the nondescript houses have been completely abandoned by man. Weeds grow tall in the front yards and forests close in behind.

Such signs of desuetude, however, only serve as a contrast to equally frequent evidences of survival. All over the State, for instance, there are . . .

EVERYWHERE THERE ARE BEAUTIFUL OLD HOUSES

... beautiful old mansions, supplemented by outbuildings which follow the same classic pattern as the main house; they are set in the midst of spacious grounds, ornamented with flower beds and blossoming shrubs, and approached by avenues of magnificent trees. None of these is more stately than Oaklawn—a typical product of the ante-bellum period—situated on Bayou Teche, between Franklin and Baldwin.

Its first owner, Alexander Porter, was a noted lawyer and a great friend of Henry Clay; the huge bathtub, cut from a single block of marble, which Mr. Porter provided for his distinguished guest, is one of the sights of the place to this day. After the War Between the States, the mansion was acquired by Colonel Rivers, the last owner of the old St. Louis Hotel in New Orleans; following the wreckage of that famous establishment, Colonel Rivers transferred some of its golden chandeliers and ornate mosaic flooring to Oaklawn, which they still adorn. But the most romantic part of its history came later still: Captain Clyde Barker, the skipper of a small steamboat, plying Bayou Teche, coveted Oaklawn from the time he was a cabin boy and saved every cent he earned. When he obtained a position of authority, he ordered the searchlights of his boat turned full on Oaklawn every time he passed it, so that his passengers and crew might get a good look at his future residence; and to make doubly sure that everyone's attention was attracted, he had the ship's bells rung at the same time. And, in due course, he did, indeed, come into possession of Oaklawn!

EVERYWHERE THERE ARE BEAUTIFUL OLD CEMETERIES

All over the state there are beautiful old cemeteries, where the people who once lived in the beautiful old houses have been reverently and fittingly laid to rest. Their great tombs are surrounded by fragrant flowers and shaded by luxuriant trees, in much the same manner as their dwelling places. The burying ground which surrounds Grace Church, in St. Francisville, is one of the most peaceful and pleasant of all these cities of the dead. It is hard to visualize it as the scene of conflict. Yet both church and church-yard suffered from shellfire during the War Between the States; and there is a story to the effect that the young Union officer in command of the gunboats on the river—himself a staunch Episcopalian—was horrified when he learned the nature of the locality he had ordered attacked.

But the beauties of a bygone age are by no means the only outstanding features along the stretches of road where our "whichaway bug" has guided us. Everywhere . . .

EVERYWHERE THERE ARE "PECKERWOOD" MILLS

. . . . there are "peckerwood" mills, operated by small stationary engines and half-hidden between the woods behind them and the piles of sawdust in front. The cutting capacity of each is only a few thousand feet a day; but their number is so great that, among them, they represent a substantial part of the State's timber harvest, which is one of its most important industries. Another aspect of the "peckerwood" mills' importance is their adaptability. They can be moved from one tract to another, as need arises, while a larger and more intricate type of mill must remain stationary.

After the lumber has been cut, it is stacked to air dry, not in flat piles, as we are accustomed to seeing it farther north, but crisscross fashion on long racks. The effect of this type of stacking—another frequent . . .

. . . feature on the landscape—is very striking; it forms an unusual pattern and it glistens in the sun, its ocher coloring vivid against a glowing sky. Most of the wood so stacked is locally used, unplaned, for cabins; also for barns, chicken houses and other outbuildings. The remainder is removed by truck to large mills, where it is dressed and finished for general use.

Another statewide industry is the . . .

... culture of bees.

Colonies of modern beehives are to be found here, there and everywhere in Louisiana, except along the immediate southern sea-rim. But most of the apiaries are not primarily devoted to the production of honey. To be sure, the blue vervain of the uplands, the tupelo gums of the swamps, the white clover that decks the levees, and the feathered blossoms of the swamp palmettos yield fabulous honey flows in their season. During the tupelo flow, for example, a single hive has been known to gain seventeen pounds during a single day; seventeen pounds of sweetness that has been brought in one microscopic droplet at a time.

The Louisiana honeys are very aromatic and full-bodied. But they are also dark, and custom decrees that the "water-white" honeys of clover and sage are what the buyers most desire. Most of Louisiana's major apiaries, therefore, are devoted to the assembly line production of royalty. In this mild climate, young, fertile and vigorous queens can be reared in February and March, ready to be shipped to Northern apiaries by the time the snows have fled and the first blossoms have appeared.

Any fertile egg laid in a beehive can become a queen. For the first three days after their hatching, all larvae are fed by their nurse bees a "royal jelly." If they were kept on this diet, they would all become queens. But, after three days, they are fed bee-bread—a mixture of pollen and honey—and develop as sexually incomplete females—or workers. Deprive a hive of its queen, and in great excitement its inmates immediately rear half a dozen larvae on royal jelly alone. The first queen to hatch—a jealous monarch—destroys the other queen cells. A few days later she makes her single mating flight, becoming "the bride of a moment and the widow of a lifetime," as the male who captures her dies in her embrace. Then she is ready to repopulate the hive and save it from extinction.

So the Louisiana queen breeder divides a swarm into small packages, places each one, with some brood-comb containing eggs, into a miniature hive, and lets the bees raise a queen. As soon as she is mated, he places her in a small cage of screen-wire and wood, plugs its only opening with candy, and ships her off to Minnesota, Wisconsin, Ohio—or to South America perhaps. Installed in her new home, her future subjects eat away the candy barrier to her prison, welcome her with caresses, and stoke her with the unbelievable quantities of food she needs to lay six eggs a minute twenty-four hours of the day to maintain a family of sixty thousand short-lived and infertile working children, whose mission it is to gather and store honey, pollinate blossoms, and serve as text for instruction into the mysteries of life.

Proceeding to the consideration of still more important industries, we will find that ...

EVERYWHERE THERE IS OIL

. . . all over the State there are oil and gas wells, some of them representing major operations, involving millions of capital invested, and others representing minor operations, involving much more modest investment. The great black derricks, which are the outward and visible sign of prospective or prevalent oil beneath the earth's surface, rise, with amazing frequency, both singly and in groups, above the level landscape. They cast long shadows across green pastures and still waters reflect their majesty. When the sun is bright, they glitter above barren places and, through the darkness, their lights shine like beacons in the midst of swamps and on the far horizon.

128

Oil was first discovered in Louisiana about fifty years ago, near Jennings, which is only twenty miles from Crowley, so that I feel I can claim Scott Heywood, who played an important part in its initial production, as a neighbor of mine. It is now found in forty-two of the sixty-four parishes, and Louisiana ranks third among the states in total production and first in production per square mile. In an average day, during 1948, 472,000 barrels of crude oil worth $1,300,000 were pumped from the earth; and now that the waters of the Gulf are also prospected and drilled, this quantity and this value have already been substantially increased.

Because of the immense potential profits, long chances are often taken in the hope that these may lead to discovery. Any wells drilled where no oil was ever produced before are known as "wildcats." They are looked upon as a great gamble, though they are perfectly legal. On the other hand, the Conservation Department sets strict limits as to the spacing of the wells and the amount of oil which may be taken from each in a given time, because a gradual withdrawal over an extended area will have better results, in the long run, than hasty, concentrated exploitation. These limits have, unfortunately, sometimes been disregarded, and when such infringements of the law are discovered, the penalty is heavy; but this has not prevented numerous persons from making large fortunes based on the so-called "hot oil."

Drilling goes on night and day and the purpose of the derrick, which indicates oil activity, is to manipulate the long pipes, which have been boring down to the oil-bearing sands, sometimes to a depth of twelve thousand feet. From the derricks the oil goes to adjacent storage tanks and from these to the refinery for processing. Transportation is accomplished by pipe line, barge or rail. The component parts of crude oil—such as gasoline, lubricants, butane and alcohol—have such diverse uses that there is very little waste. From the refinery, the oil is redistributed into consumer channels.

Besides the conveyances used for the oil itself, transportation for personnel is provided by various means. The most arresting of these is the amphibian which, in ever-increasing numbers, is used as a taxi between operations in the Gulf and land bases. In all outlying areas, the employees of the major . . .

. . . oil companies are furnished with comfortable living quarters; and in some cases, hospitalization and recreational facilities are locally provided as well. In fact, these plants often assume the aspect of neat little villages and occasionally—like the community at Destréhan—they achieve aspects of great beauty.

When an oil well is brought in as a producer, it is topped by a many-branched pipe and valve system, which acts as a regulator and a control and which is known as a "Christmas tree." Considering that the well in question has usually enabled its owner to act as Santa Claus on a large scale, the term seems singularly appropriate!

EVERYWHERE THERE ARE CATTLE

From the swampy lands of the coastal areas to the red hills of North Louisiana, great herds, which are constantly growing still greater, range over the marshes and pastures, usurping much of the marginal land formerly planted to rice, cotton and sugar. Though dairying plays an important part in the scheme of things, the larger number of these herds consist of beef cattle; and though thoroughbreds are highly valued, the main idea in connection with them is not to keep a single strain pure; it is to develop better and bigger cattle through the processes of crossbreeding.

The early settlers had herds of long-horned animals which came to Louisiana from Spain, via Mexico and Texas, and, up to the middle of the last century, these longhorns formed the dominant breed. Then experiments to improve it began. One of the first recorded instances of this experimentation was on the plantation of Dr. Bennet H. Barrow, in West Feliciana Parish. The British government had sent an agronomist there to study farming methods; a year later, this specialist returned to India. Dr. Barrow had declined to accept any payment for his hospitality, so, in appreciation of this, the Britisher ordered shipped to him four bullocks of the breed used in India for draft animals. He thought that these bulls, crossed with the native cows, would produce a larger type of draft animal, for use in cultivating the fields and logging the forests, than were then available.

These four Brahmas were considered a great novelty, attracting the attention of plantation owners and cattlemen from adjoining parishes and states. One of these gentlemen came from Texas. He so admired the great beasts with humps on their shoulders and long drooping ears that he purchased one from Dr. Barrow and took it home to breed to his native cows. From this small incident, one of the greatest foundation herds of Brahmas in the United States was developed. The progeny of the imported bull set the pattern. Their offspring grew faster and were ready to market sooner than the offspring of the longhorns. They also inherited the more favorable characteristics of both strains.

As time passed, cattlemen imported each year, in greater numbers, herd sires and dams, not only from India, but from England, choosing the most important British beef breeds. The next logical step was to develop a breed combining the best features of the imported strains. This program was worked out on the King Ranch in Texas and, after years of careful selection, the deep red-colored Santa Gertrudis cattle have been perfected there. Other ranchers have profited by this development and, at the Lake Grove Plantation, home of the David Lides, near Newellton . . .

... some of the best examples of this lengthy experiment in breed improvement can now be seen.

Lake Grove supplies almost every answer to a cattleman's dream: it is located on the banks of Lake Bruin, which insures it plentiful fresh water; its broad acres of cultivated land supplement its levee pastures. Between them, these furnish feed for ten months out of the year; in the remaining two months, unless the winter is exceptionally severe, the cattle can feed and fatten on ...

. . . buck-vine which grows in profusion among the tall cottonwood trees along the twelve miles of batture now embraced by the plantation, which has recently been greatly enlarged.

Evergreen Plantation,[13] an adjoining estate, has been acquired by the Lides and combined with Lake Grove. The addition of these new thousands of acres affords facilities, not only for the expansion of the home herds, but for the winter fattening of cattle from less fortunately situated sections of the South and Southwest.

COTTON GROWS FROM THE RED HILLS TO

THE SUGAR BOWL

As we have already learned, Louisiana's first successful experiments in cotton growing were made by the Prudhommes, near Natchitoches, early in the eighteenth century.
The invention of the cotton gin, seventy-five years later, made its general production
profitable. Its cultivation has now spread from the Red Hills of the North to the Bayou
Country of the South and it has become Louisiana's leading crop from the standpoint
of both value and acreage.

Cotton is planted from seed in the early spring, as soon as all danger of frost is past;
by the first of June, it has reached a growth of about a foot and the long straight rows,
rising above the clean earth in one field after another, are a beautiful sight. The cotton
has already been "chopped" (thinned) by hand and has undergone continuous cultivation by machinery. By late June, the cotton plant is blossoming. By August, the first
bolls have formed and opened and are ready for picking. During a favorable season,
growth and harvest continue into December.

On many of the larger plantations, cotton is now picked with mechanical harvesters. But on small farms, this is impractical, and it is done by hand, men, women and children all taking part in the operation. They are supplied with long bags, made of a canvas-like material, commercially called Osnaburg, but locally designated as loral. At its open end is a band which the pickers loop over one shoulder. With the seven-foot sacks dragging along the rows behind them, they move down the field, detaching the "locks" of cotton from their hard brown burrs. A good adult picker can average between three and four hundred pounds of seed cotton a day and, for the most part, this work is done in an atmosphere of great good cheer, to the accompaniment of story-telling, joking, laughing and singing; but should one picker in a row become upset for any reason, his feeling is quickly communicated to all the others. Poisonous snakes are not uncommon in the cotton fields—or anywhere else in Louisiana, I am sorry to say!— and the presence of a cottonmouth is quickly betrayed by its musky odor, which can usually be detected at a distance of ten or twelve feet. When it is, the alarm is quickly given, and one of the pickers volunteers to do away with the menace, which he finishes off with dexterity and dispatch. Otherwise, a fatality may very easily take place.

As the bags are filled they are taken to the scale-wagon, parked on one of the head-lands. There each is weighed, emptied and carried back to the field for refilling. When the wagon is filled, it is taken to a storehouse or direct . . .

... to the gin. There the seed cotton is sucked pneumatically into the gin stands, where the seed and the lint are separated. The lint is next pressed into bales, each weighing approximately five hundred pounds. Then it is ready for shipping.

The bales usually represent the best bet of the small farmer, who is also a landowner, for a cash crop. With two mules and a twelve-dollar plow, he can handle six acres of cotton. The yield varies. A bale to the acre is good, and not uncommon. At thirty cents a pound, each bale represents one hundred fifty dollars in cash, plus whatever is received for seed. Nine hundred dollars will go a long way toward meeting the annual needs of himself and his family. His lot is by no means a wretched one, as long as cotton prices are reasonably stable, and when the time comes for the pay-off, this marks a red-letter day. He and his family celebrate by going to town. New shoes, new calico dresses, new jeans and a supply of snuff for Grandma are all on the shopping list.

The gin operator, too, has well-being within his reach. He earns a substantial profit and has time for other pursuits, as ginning take up only about four months in the year. One gin worker, J. C. Bueche, saved his wages to buy a gin of his own; he had especially looked forward to blowing its big steam whistle—the traditional symbol of the cotton harvest. Indeed, many transactions in the cotton country are referred to as given under "gin whistle dating." This means that the debt will be discharged, the goods will be delivered, and so on, when the cotton crop is harvested and the cash comes in. Mr. Bueche had heeded the summons of the whistle for years in the gin where he was employed. Eventually, he acquired a very fine gin near New Roads, on the banks of False River. But alas! it was so completely modern that everything in it was electrically operated. He could not blow a steam whistle, because there was no steam!

139

WHERE, OF COURSE, YOU BEGIN TO GET SUGAR

By the time we have left Bueche's gin, we are beginning to see fields of sugar cane alternating with the cotton patches along our country road. Alma Plantation which, like the gin, is near New Roads, is one of the most prosperous and productive, for its size, in the State; it is not only admirably managed, but soil and climatic conditions in this area are almost ideal for a sugar crop. Poplar Grove, above Port Allen on the Mississippi, some thirty miles distant from New Roads, is another flourishing plantation; its resourceful owner, Horace Wilkinson, has tried a unique and highly successful experiment there: as soon as the cane is cultivated in the spring, sheep are turned in to graze between the rows of young shoots, and by this means the headlands are kept completely clean until harvest time. The sheep will not touch the cane itself, but they fatten on the grass, and Mr. Wilkinson, like the farmers who turn ducks into their rice fields, profits by a double crop.

In the vicinity of Poplar Grove are numerous other fine plantations, most of them distinctly modern in plant and equipment. However, the old mill at Union, now abandoned in favor of the up-to-date sugarhouse at St. Louis, is a picturesque reminder of the lush days before mosaic disease, Johnson grass and the need for artificial fertilizers came to plague the planter. The old mill at Tally-Ho, with a classic doorway worthy of any ante-bellum mansion, is another which evokes pleasant nostalgia; while the sugarhouse parties at Cora Texas and the dove dinners at Catherine still uphold and interpret the lavish tradition of the past.

At Cinclaire Central Factory, new customs are supplanting old ones, but in a gradual and practical manner: tractor-drawn carts . . .

... line up for loading at one central machine before going on to the factory; but mules still move this loader slowly from one part of the field to another. By the time the last mule has died, every phase of the harvesting operation will, no doubt, be mechanized; meanwhile, the faithful animals still play their part in the scheme of things.

The road which stretches south along the Mississippi from Port Allen to Donaldsonville, and then follows Bayou Lafourche to Raceland, is the one I know best among the many which are bordered by sugar cane. It is, therefore, perhaps natural that I should feel the most affection for it. But the so-called "Sugar Bowl" of Louisiana lies west of this, extending almost to Abbeville and embracing the rich lands around Franklin, Jeanerette, New Iberia and St. Martinville; and, at Festival time, New Iberia is still the scene of a beautiful and impressive ceremony, once general in the sugar country and now, unfortunately, almost abandoned.

This ceremony—the Blessing of the Sugar Cane—takes place the evening before actual work begins in the fields and factory. The hands, clothed in their Sunday best, line up in long rows beside the field nearest the sugarhouse with their implements, mules and carts, and all the carts are decorated ...

. . . with stalks of cane in honor of the great occasion. Everything is in readiness when the cleric begins his walk between the rows, accompanied by a crucifer, acolytes and choristers, and—if he himself is of exalted ecclesiastical rank—by the parish priest. In the train of this imposing procession come the "bossman" of the plantation, the over-seer, the chief engineer and various invited guests from neighboring plantations and near-by towns. As he progresses, the cleric bestows his blessing on everyone and every-thing he passes. He prays that the workers may be industrious, the mules patient and enduring, the knives sharp, the carts strong, the harvest plentiful. The male workers stand with bowed heads until he has gone by; they hold their hats respectfully in their hands and their dark faces glow above their white shirts. The female workers, wearing freshly starched dresses, hold their children close and hush them if they point or ask questions. Most of the Negroes are Baptists, but they hold the Catholic cleric in very high esteem; they admire his regalia and his entourage and firmly believe that his blessing will insure a good crop.

Climatic conditions are, of course, unchangeable, but the amount of human labor required to produce and harvest a ton of sugar cane has been greatly reduced in Louisiana during the last fifteen or twenty years by the design, construction and use of machines for specialized work.[14] Practically all of this development work has been done locally by local people. As a matter of fact, the work has been largely inventive, as no models existed which could be copied or improved; therefore, the mechanization of the Louisiana cane fields is almost entirely the result of native ingenuity and experimentation. Machines for plowing, cultivating and harvesting cane have been produced, and are used in Louisiana, which have counterparts nowhere else in the world, unless shipped there from this State.

A recent visit to the impressive plant of the Thomson Machinery Company in Thibodaux furnished us with a striking example of the far-flung demand for such local products. Generally, we were told by the genial executive who took us through the plant, we would see various types of cultivators and harvesters in the process of construction; but, at the moment, everything else had been set aside in order to respond to an emergency call for providing . . .

144

. . . cane cars for Madagascar. In this remote island, so we learned, the cane cars are run entirely on outsize railway tracks; the standard size cane cars in general use elsewhere are, therefore, completely impractical for Madagascar sugar growers who, perforce, require special supplies. The dispatch of such orders also represents a problem, for shipments to this outpost cannot be made frequently and easily as in the case of shipments to Puerto Rico, for example. At the time of our visit to the Thomson Company only a fortnight remained in which to fill an order representing both a major financial consideration to the manufacturer and essential harvesting equipment to a vital and dependent industry. Row after row of cane cars in various stages of manufacture, each surrounded by a crew of workmen, bore cogent witness to the determination and ability of the company to meet the challenge. The deafening noise, the sputtering sparks, the heavy helmets worn by the workers, the speed of their movements and the intensity of their application all served to heighten the drama and urgency of the scene.

PULPWOOD IS MORE LOCALIZED

Louisiana leads all other states in the production of pulpwood. This production is facilitated by the fact that fifty per cent of its land area is tree-covered, and that a large part of this arboreal growth is ready for cutting when it is fifteen years old. Besides the men who devote all their time to the pulpwood industry, many farmers, fishermen and trappers find the cutting of pulpwood a profitable seasonal occupation and pulp mills are located at strategic points throughout North Louisiana, the largest and most important being at Spring Hill, near Shreveport. There is also a very large plant at Bogalusa, in Washington Parish.

The present owners and operators of these mills regard them in a very different light from the men who ran them half a century ago, when it was customary to strip a tract and abandon it, along with the mushroom town which was allied to it. Today, each major mill has its own conservation department, which is responsible for the reforestation of the tracts it has cleared, and which also embraces in its activities assistance in the planting and replanting . . .

146

. . . of timberland belonging to others, wherever such assistance is indicated. Timber is regarded as an annual crop, like sugar, cotton or any other product of the state, and steps are taken to safeguard it and improve it with much the same underlying thoughtfulness. The ultimate aim is naturally a perpetual cut and a balanced economy.

The first proponent of scientific reforestation in Louisiana was Mr. Henry Hartner, organizer of the Urania Lumber Company in LaSalle Parish. As early as 1910 he asked the United States Forest Service to send a trained forester for consultation with himself and his associates. The request was granted and the experiments which resulted from it had far-reaching consequences. Ten years later the Great Southern Lumber Company at Bogalusa sent representatives to the Urania forest and became convinced that they could employ the methods used there to good advantage; they also originated certain methods of their own. Many other companies have followed suit and the influence of the Urania reforestation project has spread far beyond the limits of Louisiana.

AND SO IS TUNG

Those portions of Louisiana which lie east of the Mississippi and north of Lake Pontchartrain are generally known as the Florida Parishes, because they were still under the jurisdiction of Spain at the time of the Louisiana Purchase and did not become part of the United States until several years after France ceded its disputed territory. These parishes are Tangipahoa, St. Tammany, Washington, St. Helena and Livingston. They are all characterized by their fine growth of pine; and their Bogue Chitto, Tchefuncta, Tickfaw and numerous other rivers are noted for their bass fishing, which attracts many visitors. The latter is also true of St. Tammany, famous for its "Ozone Belt," where the air is supposed to possess especially invigorating qualities. As we have already observed, Bogalusa, in Washington Parish, boasts a pulp mill comparable in size and in importance to the one at Spring Hill, near Shreveport. Washington Parish is also the center for the development of a product which combines exquisite beauty with a rare degree of usefulness; and this development has an interesting story behind it.

In the early twenties Mr. Walter Green, Sr., who lives near Franklinton, became interested in tung oil production as carried on in China. He planted a few acres, where previously there had been only pine stumps, with . . .

. . . tung trees. These flourished, so he grew his own seedlings and increased his acreage. This was done in an atmosphere of considerable skepticism and ridicule, but he persevered; and when civil war in China reduced production there, he began to reap the benefits of his foresight. Following his example, others started to develop land in a similar manner throughout the Southern States in areas where a type of soil favorable to tung exists; but the amount of such soil is limited, whereas pine can be raised almost anywhere.

With the coming of World War II, the entire crop was bought by the United States Navy because tung oil is an ideal vehicle for certain types of paint. Now Mr. Green owns more than four thousand acres of productive trees. Since cattle will not eat the leaves, the ground beneath the tung trees is planted with legumes during the winter and herds are turned out to graze there. Before the nuts are harvested the stock is removed, and thus, like the rice fields and the cane fields, the tung farms provide a dual crop.

Meanwhile, the rolling countryside for miles around has been covered with snow-white blossoms, much as the Shenandoah Valley is covered with apple blossoms in the springtime. In this respect, as in some others, Louisiana can vie with Virginia in its lavish display of rare and natural beauty.

MOSS GIVES RISE TO MISTAKES

To the average outsider, Louisiana's vast swamps appear to be just so much waste-land. Nothing could be further from the truth. Besides fur-bearing animals, fish, timber and oil, the greater part of the gray moss used commercially comes from the swamps. There is also considerable misconception about moss itself; it is often regarded as a parasite, threatening the very lives of the trees which it drapes. As a matter of fact, the only thing it takes from them is support. On the other hand, it has considerable value, as it is extensively used for upholstery.

Moss is a slow-growing plant, which takes ten or fifteen years to reach a length when it can be profitably gathered. This gathering is always done with a long wooden shaft, called a moss pole, equipped with a hook at the end; but sometimes the gathering is from the top of a derrick attached to a boat; . . .

. . . sometimes from the tree itself, which the moss gatherer has climbed after the fashion of a telegraph or telephone lineman; and sometimes by breaking off the moss-draped limbs from a tree and stripping them when on the ground. The first two methods are equally good; the third is, of course, destructive and wasteful.

After it has been gathered, the moss is retted, that is, steeped in water and turned over and over again until the fleshy portions have decayed, and only the wiry black core of each filament remains. Then it is hung on long wires or fences to dry. This process takes about two weeks. After that, the moss goes to a gin, where it is cleaned, combed and baled; then it is ready to ship to the manufacturer who uses it to fill mattresses and overstuffed furniture. It does not require mixing with any other substance. It has become almost as firm and springy as horsehair. In fact, many persons think it is!

Which is another mistake that Louisianians take no particular trouble to correct!

BUGGIES STILL BELONG

Buggies cannot, strictly speaking, be called the product of Louisiana, because they are not manufactured here. But Southwestern Louisiana absorbs more than half the annual product of all the buggy makers still surviving in the United States; and, until very recently, the town's largest buggy dealer in Abbeville had a more extensive display than any automobile dealer. Rural merchants still exist who hesitate to give credit to automobile owners, but who willingly extend it to buggy owners. Buggy weddings, in which no member of the bridal party uses motor transportation to either the church or the reception, are by no means uncommon; and the "pave," instead of dropping off abruptly into marshland, so treacherous that it is not safe to turn onto it, is bordered on either side by a roadway—firm but still not too hard on hooves—so that buggies may jog comfortably along.

As we come from New Orleans to Crowley, we begin to see buggies in Opelousas and by the time we get to Carencro or Church Point—depending on which road we take—we see a good many. At Church Point the hitching rails . . .

. . . border both sides of the driveway between the church and the main road, a distance of several hundred feet; and, on Saturday afternoons, when the country folk come to Confession, and at early Sunday morning Mass—the favorite service—there is no space to spare. Scott, five miles out of Lafayette, is also a favorite center. The designers for the type of buggy prevalent in this region evidently intended it for the use of only two persons at a time; more frequently, it somehow accommodates five or six!

Its most impressive use, as far as my experience goes, was at the local premiere of Flaherty's fine moving picture, "Louisiana Story," in Abbeville. Various types of celebration preceded the showing and among these was a buggy parade. An outstanding participant was a jovial old gentleman who once journeyed all the way to Washington in his buggy, taking with him a white rooster which he bestowed on the President of the United States. On the gala occasion of the premiere, he was minus the rooster, but persistently clutched a bulky paper parcel which he would not entrust to his grandson, who drove for him, and which he took with him to Frank's Theater when his buggy, like all the others, was parked outside. The nature of its contents is a mystery to me. But I have always suspected that some descendant of the President's rooster had now progressed as far as chicken sandwiches!

GRAVEYARD WORKING
IN GRANT PARISH

I have said, quite truthfully, that all over Louisiana there are beautiful old cemeteries which bear a certain resemblance to each other. But in Grant Parish are some which are unique in themselves and also in the customs connected with them.

Every year on the fourth Saturday of May and again on the fourth Saturday of September, the people of the parish foregather to pay homage to their dead. Notices of the "graveyard working" are printed beforehand in the local papers and everyone is urged to help.

The response to this appeal is very general. Men begin to arrive at the rural graveyards about seven in the morning, most of them wearing their working clothes, and equipped with hoes, shovels and buckets for carrying water and extra earth. They chop and scrape the large areas of the graveyard, removing all grass and weeds and revealing the red ground. As they move from section to section, they discuss many things of which it is natural for men of the locality to speak—rainfall, crops and timberland, hunting and fishing and the ravages of the wild hogs which range through their woods.

The womenfolk, wearing freshly laundered print dresses, come later in the morning. They bring great baskets full of flowers and boxes full of food. The older ones move from grave to grave, recalling the persons buried in them, who was married to whom, what illnesses were fatal, and so on, as the epitaphs are slowly read aloud. The younger women help the menfolk with their work of chopping and scraping and fill the containers with flowers. After the work is done, not a blade of grass remains in the cemetery and every grave is freshly hilled, as if burials had just taken place; only the lichens and the discolorations of time betray the age of the tombstones.

When the women come, they bring their children with them and these youngsters are also spick and span; they play together, quietly, but without restraint. This graveyard working is not a sad occasion; it is one of tribute . . .

. . . by the living to the dead, paid with reverence and with a renewal of faith, but "without money and without price." No one is hired to do the work; it is a freewill offering and it is followed by an ample feast. Pews are brought out from the church which the graveyard surrounds and arranged in U formation. A blessing is asked and then everyone helps himself to the picnic lunch and eats with hearty appetite: fried chicken, fresh pork roast, bread, cakes and pies of every description. The neighborhood gossip subsides while the hungry people eat. But through the peaceful stillness come the pleasant sounds of the countryside—the crowing of a rooster on a near-by farm, the tinkle of a cowbell in a pasture, the whistle of a bobwhite in the woods, the rustle of wind through the pine trees.

Then dusk and silence, when the workers are gone and the dead are alone again.

155

THE RIVER ROAD
WAS THE ONE
I FIRST KNEW WELL

I TAKE OVER A "COTTAGE"

The first stretch of road with which I became familiar in Louisiana was the old River Road on the east bank of the Mississippi, between Baton Rouge and New Orleans. I went to live on this road, in order to acquaint myself with the locality, which I wished to use as the setting for a novel, and took up my abode in a twenty-room ante-bellum house, somewhat incongruously called "the Cottage."

The story of the Cottage has been permeated with drama from the time it was built in 1824, when Colonel Abner Duncan presented it to his daughter, Frances Sophia, on the occasion of her marriage to Frederick Daniel Conrad. It was finished in time to receive Lafayette, when he made his memorable visit to Baton Rouge; Zachary Taylor, Judah P. Benjamin and Henry Clay were frequent guests there. (The desk at which Clay wrote some of his most famous speeches and the room which he occupied are still shown with pride; and though I do not doubt their authenticity, I cannot help noting that the houses which Clay presumably visited in Louisiana are almost as numerous as the beds, enshrined all the way from Virginia to Massachusetts, in which Washington allegedly slept.) In the War Between the States, the house was taken over for a Federal Hospital; and, a few years later, it was put to similar use, because of a great and sudden disaster: the steamboat, *Princess,* loaded with sightseers to watch the famous race between the *Natchez* and the *Robert E. Lee,* caught fire slightly upstream and rescue skiffs were put out from the bank. Linen sheets were spread all over the lawn and liberally sprinkled with flour brought from the barrels in the great storerooms; and, as the victims of the explosion were brought ashore, they were rolled in these to assuage their pain until more expert care could be given them.

Like every other well-equipped Southern house, the Cottage has its ghost, and a more intriguing one than the usual headless horseman or wailing lady: in the early days of its occupancy, a Scotch tramp came up the levee at sunset; and, stopping at the Big House, asked first for a drink of water, then for a hot meal and next, for a night's lodging. He never left the place again. He called himself Angus Holt, and he proved to be an experienced landscape architect and a classical scholar, qualified to act as tutor for the planter's children. He kept his origin a secret all his life; and when he died, he was buried in the garden which was the work of his hands. It is said his spirit stills haunts it. Perhaps it does. There is an eerie quality about it, especially in the moonlight. But that is true also of the great trees, draped with white wisteria and Cherokee roses, as well as waving gray moss. I never could decide whether they were more beautiful at night, or in the late afternoon, when the sun was setting and the sky all aglow with color. I used to pace up and down the long walk, bordered by scarlet amaryllis and snowy yucca, trying to decide.

I never could. But it is the beauty of the Cottage, not any ghost which may visit it, that haunts me still.

CREACY AND KING COME INTO MY LIFE

It was when I went to live at the Cottage that Creacy and King came into my life. Everyone had told me, beforehand, that I would not be able to get anyone to work for me there, and though I had been told this before and lived to laugh it off, I was very much afraid that, this time, everyone might be right. The Cottage is only eight miles from Baton Rouge, the capital of Louisiana; but, in many ways, it is the most isolated place in which I have ever kept house. It has no telephone and no mail delivery, and, in times of high water or seepage, the winding gravel road which leads to it is more or less—oftener more than less—impassable. Since foodstuffs, not to mention drinking water, had to be brought out from Baton Rouge by car— under gas rationing!—this inaccessibility presented certain practical drawbacks which, at times, became fairly serious. I felt that my own residence there was indicated by my work, but it did not seem probable that anyone else would feel that way except Miss Clara, the faithful housekeeper, who has stood by me, through thick and thin, for twenty years now. When Steele Burden, the landscaping genius who had agreed to restore Angus Holt's garden for me, informed me that a colored couple, named Creacy and Beverly King, might be available, I was sure the hand of the Lord was in it. I am still sure of this.

Creacy and King were then living in a small near-by shack and, except for intermittent work by the day, they were unemployed. (This in itself was a minor miracle in the early Spring of 1944.) The shack was, of course, without plumbing or electricity and was in a generally tumble-down condition. The roof leaked so badly that, every time it rained, Creacy and King had to move their bed and the building stood on undrained land, so that in wet weather they had to put on high boots whenever they left it. They had some chickens and turkeys, . . .

158

... a few cows, a mule and a small garden patch of their own. They had seen better days and subsequent experience leads me to believe that, even then, they were "better fixed" than they appeared to be, for both have thrifty habits and know how to "put away bales of cotton without breaking their backs." But, to me, their situation seemed deplorable.

King started work almost immediately; that is to say, he moved about the place in an unhurried manner, his brow shielded by a tattered felt hat which he never changed with the seasons. He believed in rest periods for every day of the week and he always remembered the Sabbath to keep it holy. But, in an amazingly short time, the driveway lost its abandoned look, the flower garden ...

. . . began to regain much of its eerie charm, and even the path leading to the cemetery where the Yankee soldiers were buried—a path long overgrown with vines and rank weeds—was cleared for passage to the old burying ground, where order and seemliness had also been restored. Nor was this all. He spoke gently to the dogs and they loved him. He sang old spirituals at parties in a way that moved Northern visitors to tears. And when he was stricken with appendicitis and I did what little I could to make the ordeal of his operation easier, he revealed a capacity for gratitude that went straight to my heart. "You sure is a post in my life fence," he told me from his sickbed. "And I ain't never gwine to forget it." By that time he had become a strong support to my own design for living.

All growing things respond to King's care in the way that they do only for those who have real feeling for them. He would not be happy out of a garden or deprived of the fowl and animals which he believes belong with it. But his greatest and deepest attachment is for his wife. He shows this attachment in a dozen different ways and is completely lost if he is separated from her for more than a few days at a time. Every morning since their marriage years ago, he has risen before she did, fetched her water with which to rinse her mouth and then made the coffee which he brings to her bedside. Not until she has drunk it, does Creacy think of stirring herself.

Perhaps this is one of the reasons I like her so much too. She is almost the only person I have met in Louisiana who does not make me feel like a sluggard because I am not up and about before dawn. And it is just as well I am not. If I were, I would not have Creacy to look after me. And I should now regard this as a major calamity.

The first time she came to see me she looked exactly like what you might expect of anyone who lived in a shack like hers. She had on felt slippers and a dingy wool dress; a turban, which had once been pink, was wound tightly about her head. But she had a pleasant and intelligent face. I thought so from the moment I saw her, and when she smiled and said, yes ma'am, she would come and try, she looked wonderful to me. The next morning, when she came into my room, bearing my breakfast tray, I saw that this was decorated with early roses. I remarked that it seemed to be a pretty day. "Yes, ma'am, such days is well accepted," Creacy responded. I thought so too.

Within a week . . .

. . . she had on a neat uniform, was waiting on table acceptably, turning down my bed at night and ministering, unreminded, to my insatiable taste for ice water. With this much and some other details of service, I have had something to do. (Creacy "takes heed" when I tell her something.) But I have never had to teach her how to arrange flowers much better than I can. I have never had to teach her how to make rolls that "float right off your plate" or shrimp gumbo that would "make you pure bite your fingers." I have never had to teach her to do fine laundry work. ("Ah has taken it away and washed it *good*," she has told me more than once, referring to some item with which I had attempted to cope myself.) I have never had to teach her to "raise" litter after litter of turbulent puppies. What is most important of all, I have never had to teach her to care for me, kindly and efficiently, when I am ill, or to comfort me, patiently and lovingly, when I am unhappy.

Like all of us, Creacy has her little peculiarities. Every now and then she is smitten with a headache, from which she requires time to "cool off." Meanwhile, she binds her head up as tightly as possible. If she is not careful, "a bone opens" in her wrist, and then she ties a string around her arm, so that the bone will close again. She spends endless hours cleaning woodwork, including window frames, but it gives her a "swimmin' in de head" to wash the windows themselves. ("Somebody else got to do de glasses," she told me from the beginning and I, supposing she referred to part of the tableware, was very much startled. I am still puzzled by the strange inconsistency of the causes of the swimming sensation.) And though Creacy's wages have been raised regularly, ever since she came to me, she seems to lack the wherewithal for what she needs now even more acutely than she did when she was living in the shack. However, she is discreet in her reference to these wages. "How much does Mrs. Keyes pay her help?" an inquisitive visitor once asked her. "Accordingly," Creacy replied . . .

. . . calmly and went her own way.

   She adores my cocker spaniel, Lucky, and always finds some good reason why I should not take the dog with me when I go to New Orleans from Crowley, where I established another writing center after leaving the Cottage. "Lucky need her extra-size," Creacy informed me one time conclusively. "Iffen you don't leave her here, how she gwine get it?" . . . "Go on, you know she's overweight now," I countered. . . . "That's just what Ah'se tellin' you, Mrs. Keyes," Creacy insisted. "Lucky need to run around de yard and get her extra-size." I gave in when a light dawned on me and I realized Creacy was talking about exercise. This is by no means the only occasion when she has played Mrs. Malaprop with success.

   I see that, without preamble, I have referred to the presence of Creacy in Crowley. I should have explained that, when I left the Cottage, she and King did too. It was as simple as that. It seemed perfectly natural to them—and to me—that they should.

All hail the power of Jesus' name!
Let angels prostrate fall;
Bring forth the royal diadem,
And crown Him Lord of all.

Creacy is very religious. She is meticulous in her observance of Communion Sunday and she derives great enjoyment from church suppers and missionary meetings. But she sets special store by a baptism. This is the way she described one to me.

"First we gathers in our church wid de candidates in de front row an' our preacher reads de openin' an' a chapter in de Bible an' asks his candidates questions an' dey answers. Nex' de Sister Stewards puts de gowns on de womens an' binds dey heads wid a white cloth; same time de Deacons, what we calls de Elder Brothers, ties white pocket handkerchiefs 'round de arms of de mens, right over dey suits. Nex', before we leaves for de river or de bi'a[15] or de pool or wheresoever we's gwine, we prays for de folks gwine down into de water and we sings one song, such as, 'All Hail de Power of Jesus' Name.' Den we all marches down to de river or de bi'a or de pool wid our preacher for our leader, an' we groups ourselves on de bank. Nex' we sings another hymn, such as, 'Precious Lord, Come an' Take My Hand,' an' we continues to sing it while de preacher goes down into de water wid two Elder Brothers. We keeps right on a-singin' it until de baptizin' is all over. De singin' sounds sweet an' it takes away fear.

"De first candidate dat has answered de preacher in de church is de first to be baptized an' dey comes along, one after de other, same as dey did before. When dey goes down in de water, de preacher raises up he right arm, wid a pocket handkerchief in he hand, an' he say, 'Sister Jane—or Brother John—or whatsoever—by your faith Ah baptizes you in de name of de Father an' de Son an' de Holy Ghost.' Den he put he arm under dey shoulder, de Elder Brothers helpin' him, an' he puts his hand over dey mouth an' nose so dey won't choke an' 'merses dem in de water. Nex' he bring de baptized person up so he stan' at de edge of de water an' de nex' one is dere waitin' to go in.

"De baptized person goes up de bank wid a great shout an' de Sister Stewards is ready to wrap sheets, or blankets iffen it's cold rounds de womens an' de Deacons is ready to wrap de mens. Den we goes off to a neighbor's house to dress an' back to de church an' gives de right hand of fellowship to mens an' womens too. Afterwards, we all has Communion an' de preacher reads de Law of de Church dat we has to go by. Den we sings some more, such as, 'Nearer My God to Thee,' an' before we dismiss, we goes round shoutin' an' rejoicin' because we gains so many for our church."

BUT JACK BELONGS TO THE COTTAGE

Creacy and King, as I have indicated, soon developed the feeling that they and I belonged together—a feeling which I shared. There was, however, a third member of the staff, who belonged and still belongs very definitely to the Cottage itself.

He was always called Jack, though—as I rather tardily discovered—his real name is Si Pack. For years, he had acted as caretaker at the otherwise empty house and had taken tourists around it, reciting, with a great warmth of feeling, the story he had been taught to tell. He loved to linger by the antiquated sugar kettle, like the one used by Etienne de Bore, explaining its former use. This kettle supplemented our meager water supply for the grounds and he made moderate use of it; but he did not excel as a gardener, because he found it hard to distinguish between flowers and weeds. However, he washed the "glasses" uncomplainingly, kept the open fires going, swept the walk and galleries and, indeed, performed every appointed task with an almost pathetic eagerness to please. On the rare occasions when he left the place to do "grocery shopping," he rode a shaggy old pony named Nostar. (Star had been the name selected for it before its arrival, but since it did not have the expected hexagonal spot on its forehead, it was called Nostar instead.) If Jack chanced to meet me on one of these excursions, he bowed, sweeping off his battered old hat almost to the ground. His general demeanor was equally deferential. But his attitude was a tribute to the Cottage, rather than to me.

He lived in a shack no bigger or better than the one occupied by Creacy and King, and much more crowded. About once a year he made the anxious announcement that Minta, his wife, had been rushed to the hospital, as she was developing a tumor. Eventually she would return and Jack would assure us that, after all, she was merely *comme ci, comme ca.* (I never heard him say anything else in French, but he pronounced these words glibly.) Shortly thereafter, Minta would have another baby. As I recall it, there were nine or ten children in the little shack when I arrived at the Cottage and twelve or thirteen when I left; but after awhile I lost count. Since then, there have been some more and one of them is named for me. I have taken appropriate action, the more gladly since Jack's financial resources were always extremely slender. When I took up my residence at the Cottage, he had been supporting his family on eight dollars a week, plus half the money received in tourist fees. But when I invited his children to come and share our Christmas tree, they all arrived shining with cleanliness and very neatly dressed. Moreover, their manners would have been a credit to such an assembly anywhere.

When Miss Clara and King and Creacy and Lucky and I finally left the Cottage, we also left Jack, who had helped, sorrowfully but efficiently, with our preparations for departure. He stood beside the colonnade and waved goodby to us; there had never been any question of his going too. Eventually, his elder children began to earn good wages, and when one of them secured an especially well-paying position, Minta and the others went to live with him. But Jack has stayed on at the Cottage— alone. As I said before, he belongs to the place rather than to any person; I have known other cases like that.

LONGHORNS AND INDIGO—SURVIVORS OF
THE FIRST CATTLE AND THE FIRST CROP

Creacy and King and Jack told me a great many stories, and eventually some of these found their way into the novel I was writing. But I had to seek out most of my material, and I found that one of the best ways of getting it was to travel over the old River Road, rather than over the new Airline, whenever I went between Baton Rouge and New Orleans.

It keeps close to the levee almost all the way and, from the beginning, I loved the levee—its form, its verdure, its wildflowers, the unity it creates between land and river. Some times there are stretches when no sign of life appears on it; these give a sense of great serenity. More often, its slopes are used as grazing lands and its summit is a well-traveled track for both men and beasts. The creatures which appear on it seem absorbed by it, except when they are silhouetted against the sky; then, briefly, they dominate it.

The old houses which once formed part of the Grand Parade are probably the last of their kind and represent a way of living which is almost gone; it seems appropriate that the native longhorn, once the most prevalent breed of cattle in Louisiana, but now fast disappearing, should also still survive along the River Road.

Another survivor is indigo. It is now wild and untended, and though beautiful to behold, no longer serves any useful purpose except as fodder. Nevertheless, it was the State's first important export crop. It had been extensively cultivated in the West Indies long before the settlers in Louisiana made the agreeable discovery that it would thrive equally well here; but they acted promptly upon this. Commercial manufacture of the dye was begun by Father Nicholas Beaubois, a Jesuit priest, in 1754; and soon thereafter nearly half a hundred planters were devoting themselves to the production of indigo and raising over eighty thousand pounds of it annually. It was an immensely profitable and truly magnificent crop; planters grew rich on it and travelers, who paused to admire the wonderful waving fields, wrote home about them with enthusiasm. But after some forty years of prosperity, a plague of caterpillars destroyed the harvest and Etienne de Bore, one of the wealthiest indigo growers on the river, sought about for a substitute crop. When he succeeded in granulating sugar, indigo culture in Louisiana was doomed. The second string to the bow proved the better of the two.

A STOREHOUSE BECOMES A RESIDENCE

Among my first friends on the River Road were the Gianellonis, who live at Longwood, a plantation about six miles below the Cottage. The Big House was built during
the Spanish Occupation and has the pleasing characteristics of the period; but an old
sugar storehouse which has been converted into an artistic home is even more intriguing, from my point of view. Probably no one would ever have thought of making
such an experiment if it had not been for a will which left the Big House to a married
daughter and a large part of the land to a married son. The son wished to remain on
the plantation and the two families, though good friends, realized that they were more
likely to remain so if they did not try to live together. So "S. J." bethought himself
of the storehouse and went off to consult an architect.

The results of this consultation are so happy that they ought to inspire many other
persons to similar undertakings. The main part of the storehouse has become the
family living room; it reveals the original beautiful big timbers, is open to the original
roof, and has an enormous fireplace; its furnishings give it comfort as well as character.

My next stopping place on the River Road is usually at the Church of St. Gabriel. The church itself is unremarkable; but the sidewalk leading from this to the rectory, and the rectory steps repay close inspection. Both sidewalk and steps are made from the unclaimed tombstones of a cemetery, whose abandonment was brought about by a necessary change in the position of the levee, because of a corresponding change in the river's course. Nearly all the inscriptions are in French or Spanish; many of them date back to the eighteenth century; and the names and sentiments recorded on them provide a treasure trove to a writer who is always wondering what to call her characters and how to visualize their outstanding qualities. Every time I go back to St. Gabriel's I see something I never saw before, and several of the leading characters in my books owe their creation to this persistent inspection. Not that one needs to be a novelist to enjoy St. Gabriel's; any *aficionado* of epitaphs would get a great deal out of it or, as far as that goes, anyone with a feeling for old customs, old expressions and old places. And that means a large proportion of those who love to linger on the River Road. If they did not have such a feeling, they would take the Airline instead.

Just below St. Gabriel's the road divides for the second time,[16] forming a loop with one side longer than the other and open at both ends.

The side to the right of the traveler, as he proceeds south, goes around Point Clair, following every curve of the river; the side at his left provides a short cut and, turning abruptly, meets the levee again head on. The left branch is in much more general use; in fact the right branch is so little traveled that it is half overgrown with grass and, in places, becomes so narrow that there is hardly room for one car to advance along it, much less to pass another. However, no one really knows the River Road until he has taken it, not only because this grassy byway has a charm all its own, but because it is the one which leads to . . .

Ici reposent
JOSEPH BLANCHARD,
décedé le 29 Avril 1850.
SOSTHÈNE B.
son fils décedé le 6 Novembre 1829
MARIE AURÉLINE B.
sa fille décédée le 26 Aout 1838
Souvenir de la famille.

Cher Père, modèle de probité d'affection paternelle
de douceur et d'industrie; ami et citoyen, regretté
de tous, tu vivras dans le coeur surtout de celui
qui sent le plus ta perte, & qui s'efforcera d'
t'imiter. Ton fils Surville Blanchard.

Requiescant in peace.

CARVILLE—EPITOME OF PROGRESS AND TRIUMPH

. . . United States Public Health Station No. 66, otherwise known as the National Leprosarium, near Carville.

This is the only Leper Colony in the United States. It became a Federal project in 1921, largely through the efforts of the late Senator Ransdell of Louisiana, who had labored long and faithfully toward that end; but the same location had already been used, as a haven for victims of Hansen's Disease (leprosy) by the State of Louisiana for nearly a quarter of a century. In 1894, eight persons were conveyed from the "pest house" in New Orleans to the Old Indian Camp Plantation in Carville. The transfer marked an improvement in the wretched lives of these people, but their lot was still a tragic one. They were taken up the river by night, on an old coal barge, because both the railroad and the river steamers refused them transportation; the original slave cabins on the place were the only shelter they found at the end of their journey; and, for two years, they received nothing but rudimentary and intermittent care. Then four sisters of the Order of St. Vincent de Paul volunteered to take charge of them and moved into the half ruined plantation house.

Ever since, the record of Carville has been one of progress and triumph. Before the Federal Government took over the plant, the State had already made great improvements in it. The plantation house had been restored to its status of a comfortable home, the slave cabins had been replaced by modern cottages and there were decent accommodations for a hundred patients. By 1924 there were four times that number of inmates and proper facilities to take care of them; a hospital, a recreation hall and various other buildings had been erected, including twenty-two additional cottages, where patients could be given private rooms, each equipped with running water. The nursing, medical and clerical staffs were correspondingly increased.

Probably no such thing as a perfect institution exists. But Carville comes amazingly close to it. It has its own power plant, its own fire department and its own dairy. It publishes its own monthly magazine, significantly called *The Star*. It provides for dances, concerts, motion pictures, golf, tennis, baseball, "book learning," and various types of occupational therapy. Visitors are permitted and patients are allowed to go home in cases of emergency, if the medical officer in charge has sound reason to feel they will not prove a menace to public health. There is no restriction on telephone calls or on mail, though all material leaving the colony is sterilized. River steamers give three long blasts as they pass the Leprosarium and the inmates wave and cheer in response. It is a happy custom, symbolic of the fact that they have not forgotten the world and that it has not forgotten them.

Prior to 1941, Hansen's Disease was generally treated with Chaulmoogra Oil; since then three derivatives of the sulphone family have been extensively used; and in an article by Ken Gormin, published July 17, 1949, by the *Times Picayune,* appears the announcement that . . .

. . . "SULPHONE DRUGS ARE WINNING LONG FIGHT AGAINST LEPROSY."

During the fiscal year, ending that month, fifty-two patients were discharged as "arrested" (noninfectious), by far the greatest number in any given year. According to Mr. Gormin, Dr. Frederick A. Johansen, the medical director of the Leprosarium, "cautiously but confidently" predicts that "the number of patients who will be discharged as arrested can be expected to increase as time goes on. . . . We are undertaking programs to make the patients as happy and their lives as pleasant as is humanly. possible," [17] the doctor concluded.

The attitude epitomized in this statement, even more than the fine plant and the medical progress, seems to me the supreme triumph of Carville. Here the leper has ceased to be an outcast and a pariah and has been reinvested with the great American prerogatives of life, liberty and the pursuit of happiness. On that secluded, grassy stretch of the River Road, which few travelers ever take, has been enacted one of the great epics in the history of our country. I wish Father Damien could have known about it. I think he would have been especially moved by the story of Major and Mrs. Hornbostel.

They formerly lived in Manila, where he was connected with a mining company which had offices there. He had previously been a non-commissioned officer in the Marines, and at the outbreak of World War II he entered the Army, where he became a Major in the Corps of Engineers. Both he and his wife were captured during the conquest of the Philippines; he was in the Death March to Bataan and she was interned at Santo Tomas. It was four years before they were reunited. Then he retired from the Army and they had a happy homecoming to San Francisco. But this happiness was short-lived; examination revealed that Mrs. Hornbostel had contracted leprosy during her imprisonment. It was in its early stages, but the dread signs were unmistakable. Commitment to Carville was the inevitable verdict.

174

Major Hornbostel immediately applied for commitment with her, appealing not only to the usual authorities, but even to the Surgeon General and to General Mac-Arthur. He had already been separated from his wife throughout the war, he said; he could not face another such separation. In spite of his moving argument, his plea was refused on the ground that no one may live within the inclosure except the patients and the staff. But he was permitted to work out a substitute arrangement. He bought two little cottages, one at the Leprosarium for her and one on the River Road for himself. Very early every morning he left his tiny isolated house and trudged down the grassy byway to spend the day with his wife; every evening he trudged home again, or rather back again—for, with his help, it was her abode which had become their real home. There they worked together and rested together. For her sake he shut himself off completely from the outside world, but she led an active life, contributing regularly to *The Star* and taking part in various community projects. The doctors said there was every hope that some day she would be discharged. And early in September of '49 that day came. Then the little house on the River Road was not lonely any more. It overflowed with joy such as seldom comes to any human habitation and soon thereafter the happy couple left it together, headed for New York and a fresh start on a new life. But that lonely stretch of the River Road has a new significance and a new beauty. It has been the scene of one of the most touching love stories of all time.

ALONG THE GRAND PARADE—RUINS AND REVIVALS

Not unnaturally, I shall always think of the Cottage as the most beautiful house on the River Road and the one with the most romantic history. But there were many others in the Grand Parade and every one of them has its own splendor and its own story.

There is Belle Helène,[18] which follows much the same architectural pattern as the Cottage and which moreover has, in front, an unobstructed view of the levee, over an expanse which was once a terraced garden and, at the side, a magnificent grove of live oaks. It was once the home of Duncan Kenner, Confederate Minister Plenipotentiary to Europe under Jefferson Davis, and later both a member of the United States Tariff Commission and Chairman of the Cotton Centennial in New Orleans. There is the Colomb house, a square one-story building with intriguing appendages, whose designer and builder—Dr. Christophe Colomb, Jr.—persisted in practicing dentistry despite all efforts to turn him into a planter, but who, as a sideline, made experiments which resulted in transforming bagasse[19] from a waste material to a use-

ful commercial product. There is the Hermitage—another classic example of the Greek Revival style—where, after a windstorm had blown down one of the large oaks, a carved chest was disclosed, embedded in a hollow which a slave had hewn as a hiding place for jewels and silver during the War Between the States.

Unfortunately, the Hermitage, like the Zenon Trudeau house—the only one of whose history I have been able to learn next to nothing—is in an advanced state of disintegration. The indigo is gone, but a bigger and better crop has supplanted it; the longhorn cattle are fast disappearing, but crossbreeding with Brahma stock has produced a strain more immune to insects and heat. When the old houses are gone, however, what will—or can—take their place? The Hermitage and the Zenon Trudeau house are by no means the only ones on the Grand Parade which will soon be past all help. And besides private residences, there are . . .

... such noble educational centers as St. Michael's Convent and Jefferson College to take into serious consideration.

St. Michael's Convent was the second house founded by the Society of the Sacred Heart in Louisiana. (The first was Grand Coteau, established only a year earlier, which has been in continuous operation ever since and which has expanded into a college.) For a century, the daughters of the rich planters along the River Road received their education at St. Michael's; then the nuns withdrew from it. A severe storm was a contributing cause; so, no doubt, was the fact that there were few rich planters left in the vicinity. The convent was successively used as a refuge for Mexican nuns and their pupils and as a center for the National Youth Administration. Afterward it was abandoned and since it has been demolished. The once lovely garden is now over-grown with rank grass; the beautiful columns have disappeared. In France this building would have been classed as a *monument historique* and its destruction would have been prevented by the State, even if the Church, usually so wise in such matters, had consented to it. Has Louisiana perhaps still something to learn from her Mother Country? I do not criticize or judge; I only ask.

178

The question becomes even more urgent when Jefferson College is its subject.
There is no façade with which I am familiar that presents a more dazzling effect
than this one, when the sun shines on its multiple columns, or that gives such a
sense of ethereality when these alternately emerge and disappear through a mist
rising from the river. On either side of the great iron entrance gates are small square
buildings, also adorned with columns, which presumably were once used as lodges;
and at the left of the campus is the old rectory, generally known as the "Priest's
House," another architectural gem. In the rear are several supplementary buildings
and an exquisite Gothic chapel, built by the fabulous Valcour Aime as a memorial
to one of his daughters, at the time when he took over the original secular college,
which had gone bankrupt, and presented it to the Marist Fathers. In 1927 they closed
it as an educational institution, but a few years later the Jesuits acquired it, renamed
it Manresa House and transformed it into a retreat. As such, it has given peace of
mind and strength of spirit to many. But persistent rumors indicate that it may share
the fate of St. Michael's. I can only hope that they are not true.

179

There is a brighter side to the picture of the Grand Parade. Not all the beautiful old buildings on it are in a state of disintegration or threatened with outright demolition. There are several happy exceptions. Among these is the Houmas House, generally called Burnside, and Bocage Plantation.[20] The former has been purchased by Dr. George Crozat, a distinguished representative of one of Louisiana's oldest families; the latter by his sister, Anita, also a practicing physician and a most remarkable woman, and her husband, the scholarly Dr. E. G. Kohlsdorf, formerly of Wisconsin.

Bocage was built by the first Christophe Colomb—that is, the first to come to Louisiana!—father of the dentist who experimented so successfully in bagasse. He claimed descent from the discoverer of America and, as far as I know, the claim has never been successfully disputed; but he himself came to this country, not for purposes of exploration, but to escape the guillotine. He married Francoise Bringier, whose family was long one of the most prominent on the River Road, owning the Hermitage, to which I have already referred, and Tezcuco, which, for the time being, I shall have to pass by—regretfully, for . . .

. . it is one of the most charming of all. But we cannot see everything in one trip.

Dr. Kohlsdorf has now retired from active practice and his well-earned leisure permits him to spend much of his time at Bocage. Not that this time is passed in idleness. On the contrary, little by little, without undue haste or undue expenditure, he is playing an active part in its intelligent restoration. He is ably assisted in this undertaking by Francois Chauvin, a master carpenter who comes rightly by his skill, for his father before him plied the same trade, with the same aptitude. Day after day, he and Dr. Kohlsdorf work patiently and constructively side by side. If every one of the houses on the Grand Parade, now facing ruin, could have had the same understanding and devoted attention, it is probable that few would be past redemption at the present time.

Dr. Crozat's more strenuous life does not permit him to spend as much time at Burnside as Dr. Kohlsdorf spends at Bocage; nevertheless, he has accomplished wonders there, over week ends. His was the first house on the River Road at which I was hospitably received. I little thought, that pleasant afternoon early in '42, that the River Road was to become an integral part of my own life. But I do not doubt that this pleasant visit was the first link in the chain of events that brought about my sojourn and my story.

PERIQUE TOBACCO GROWS NOWHERE ELSE
IN THE WORLD

I have said, quite sincerely, that the old houses along the River Road fascinate me more than any other feature it possesses. But I recognize that it is distinguished by other characteristics and one of these is unique. This is perique tobacco, which has been called the greatest mystery crop in the world—and no wonder. In spite of repeated efforts to raise it elsewhere, it flourishes only on a triangular piece of land skirting the Mississippi for about ten miles between Convent and LaPlace and thrusting its third point back into the swamps about three miles distant.

This strange tobacco was first raised by the Indians, who were already growing it when the Acadians came to St. James Parish in 1776. One of these settlers, Pierre Chenet, saw its commercial possibilities and began to exploit them. Among his friends, Chenet was generally called Perique, just as a man called Peter is often called Pete by his intimates. The nickname became associated with the product Chenet sold so successfully and it has been called perique tobacco ever since. It is very black and very strong and is used almost entirely for blending with milder types. The English like it and Great Britain is its best market, though a good deal is also sold in both Canada and Norway.

Like the strawberry crop, perique is a family one; fathers, mothers, and children all co-operate in its production. It is sown between Christmas and New Year's, from seeds so tiny that these have to be mixed with ashes to prevent too much concentration in the seed beds, which are protected by cold frames. The seedlings are transplanted to the fields between the middle of March and the middle of April, the plants being placed five and one-half feet apart; by late June the crop is ready to harvest. Meanwhile, cultivation has taken place and an interesting phase of this is the special work assigned to children; they are responsible for breaking off enough suckers from each stalk so that not more than twelve leaves will remain; this is necessary to insure both their size and their strength. A large amount of Chilean nitrate is used for side dressing and the crop is kept scrupulously clean by hand-hoeing and tractor-drawn discs.

When the crop is mature, it is cut by hand with a cane knife, in the early morning while the dew is still on it. It is then rushed on flat-bed trucks to the drying sheds and unloaded beneath a canopy, to protect it from the sun. Eightpenny nails are next driven into the butts of the stalks by women workers, who afterward suspend them on wires, where they remain for about two weeks. Male workers remove the dried stalks from the wires and . . .

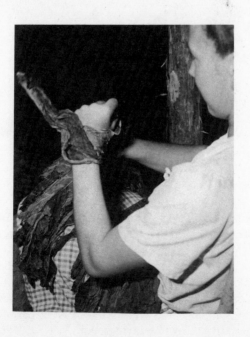

. . . beat them on wooden logs to remove the accumulated dust. Then they strip the leaves from the stalks and moisten them under a very fine spray, before turning them back to women workers, who sit at long tables and, by surprisingly deft flicks of the wrists, remove the central spines. The leaves, having been thus treated, are assembled into small bundles bound with raffia, and dropped into oaken barrels which are removed to the warehouses for curing under pressure, each barrel being equipped with a powerful jackscrew. The entire process takes two years, but, at the end of the first, the pressed tobacco is reworked by handling, turning and rearranging. When it is ready for shipping, it is transferred to fresh barrels, lined with waxed paper, each with a capacity of five hundred pounds.

Almost the entire crop of perique is controlled by two families, the Roussels, who are both planters and dealers, and the Guglielmos, who are largely dealers. Mr. Farrell Roussel grows sugar cane in large quantities to supplement his crop of perique, and Mr. J. F. Guglielmo is the principal of the Lutcher High School, so he too has varied interests and varied activities. Incidentally, he and his wife are greatly given to hospitality, and a meal at their house which includes a matchless dish of fresh river shrimp and butter beans is a feast fit for the gods. Opinions may differ about the flavor of perique tobacco; some are bound to be unfavorable, for it bears much the same relation to milder types that tabasco does to cream gravy. But there cannot possibly be two schools of thought regarding the superlative merits of shrimp stew à la Guglielmo!

CHRISTMAS EVE ON THE RIVER ROAD

Christmas Eve is a good time to drive along the River Road. Of course, any time is good, as far as that goes, but there is a special reason why it is interesting to make the trip on Christmas Eve.

For some days, in the sections around Union and Lutcher, the Negroes have been piling driftwood and roseau reeds on the levee for their Christmas bonfires. The wood is stacked around tall central poles, which look like trees, and when the reeds begin to burn, the joints explode and make a crackling noise. The bonfires give forth a lovely light and the sound that comes from them is lively, not unlike the one made by firecrackers.

If you are in the vicinity anyway, it is not a bad idea to drop in at St. Peter's Church for Midnight Mass. Naturally, you can go to Mass almost anywhere along the River Road; St. Michael's—the church, not the deserted convent—is another interesting place to choose, from a sightseeing point of view, because of the Lourdes Grotto made of Dr. Colomb's bagasse clinkers. But I have a special reason for suggesting St. Peter's at Reserve—which owes its name to a dramatic episode which had an even more dramatic sequel. The first Godchaux who went to this settlement, which was then the location of the Boudousquie Plantation, was a peddler who was repelled with extreme rudeness at the Big House. As he took his forced departure, he called back over his shoulder that the family had better "reserve" a place for him, as some day he would return with money enough to buy the plantation and dispossess the owners. Which is exactly what he did do! And he called his property Reserve!

St. Peter's is a very beautiful little church, with a façade which is even more white and glistening than the colonnade at Jefferson College; and, above the portico is a fine rose window, which was installed there as a memorial to a later Godchaux, Edward. Of course, all of Reserve is a memorial to the Godchaux family—the refinery, the schools, the playgrounds, the model quarters for employees; they have been great philanthropists as well as great sugar planters. But, in a way, the rose window is the most significant part of the memorial; for St. Peter's is a Catholic church and Edward Godchaux was a Jew.

All too often tolerance is just something people talk about, rather glibly, instead of with a sense of deep inner conviction; respect and admiration for forms of faith which are different from our own are rarer still. But there is a wise, old saying to the effect that he who knows only his own religion knows none at all. If our own belief is sincere and strong, it will not be shaken by the contemplation of other beliefs; on the contrary, it will gain in meaning for us by thoughtful and intelligent comparison. The citizens of Reserve and its parish priests have set an example through their rose window which many an other community would do well to follow.

That is why I think St. Peter's is a good place to go for Midnight Mass. On leaving the altar rail, after Communion, the worshipper will walk toward the rose window. And who knows? He may see a star, like the one over Bethlehem, shining through it.

DESTRÉHAN—A REFINERY AND A REINCARNATION

The last of the fine old houses to which we come on the River Road, going from Baton Rouge to New Orleans, is Destréhan.

It was built around the beginning of the nineteenth century by the wealthy Creole who gave it his own name. Besides being a successful merchant and planter, he was a member of the Territorial Legislature and helped draft the first State Constitution. According to tradition, Jean Lafitte was one of his frequent visitors, though what the two could have had in common is more or less of a mystery; it is still more of a mystery why the pirate should have wished to bring part of his treasure here, if indeed he did. At all events, Destréhan's alleged ghost is Lafitte. "His disconsolate shadow is said to haunt the house, appearing on stormy nights. At such times it comes from nowhere, points its finger at the hearth on the ground floor, then disappears."[21]

Destréhan has a high, sloping roof, and is architecturally more suggestive of a Norman chateau than any other plantation house in Louisiana with which I am familiar. Both the house and the grounds are kept in superb condition. Credit for this is due to the Pan American Oil Company, which virtually owns and controls the town named for the plantation and which uses the plantation house as a social center for its employees, who are all comfortably quartered in the vicinity.

The happy fate of Destréhan as compared to Esperance and Pecan Grove—to mention only two in the locality—has led me to do a little dreaming. Suppose some individual or organization should become interested in the Grand Parade, somewhat after the same manner that the Rockefellers have interested themselves in Williamsburg, for instance? There is still much more left to build on here than there was there; and while that re-embodied an ancient, beautiful and historic seat of government, a restoration of the Grand Parade would epitomize a way of life which played a significant part in our civilization and had a far-reaching effect upon it.

"A few yards from the water runs a beautiful road, bordered on one side by gardens and houses and on the other by the River. . . . The whole line of shore . . . is a continued unbroken street. . . . This . . . is the *River Road,* following in and out every curve of the embanked shore and level as a race-course track. Thus, one riding along this road has constantly the green bank, or levee, on one side, with the mile-wide river flowing majestically by. . . . On the other hand are hedges separating gardens, lawns, cottages, villas . . . with groups of live oaks, magnolias, lemon and banana trees interspersed. For miles, all the day long, the traveler can ride through a scene of beauty and ever lively interest."[22] This is the way the Grand Parade appeared to a visitor ninety years ago. What a monument to the group or individual responsible for its restoration to some semblance of its former glory, such a reincarnation would be! . . .

But for the moment, we have done both enough sightseeing and enough philosophizing. When we leave Destréhan, we will be only a short distance from the Bar-None Ranch, where there is always a warm welcome awaiting us. We will drop in for a look at the palominos and a big bowl of crayfish bisque. Then on to New Orleans and Beauregard House—"and so to bed!"

THE AIRLINE

STRAWBERRY TIME

Beginning early in April, the traveler along the Airline, between Baton Rouge and New Orleans, is inevitably arrested by the sight of a succession of young vendors, who stand close to the roadside and offer him strawberries, with a beguiling smile.

In Louisiana, strawberries are mulched with dry pine needles, and the region that stretches away from the Airline towards Hammond, the great strawberry center, is rich in its growth of pine. One-, two- and three-acre tracts lend themselves readily to the hand-grown strawberry crop; and the cabins glimpsed from the road are set in the midst of just such tracts, with a background of dense forest, which yields not only the necessary needles, but . . .

. . . offers an effective shelter from frost. Strawberry growing is essentially a family affair and the public school authorities so recognize it; children in the strawberry belt are given their vacation during the springtime, so that they can contribute their share to their parents' means of livelihood. Then, in the summer, when other children are free to "fish and fiddle" they are back at their benches. But no one who has found their smiles irresistible, and has gone on to an eventual destination with a berry-laden car, regrets the untimeliness of the holiday.

The children not only act as vendors; they also do a considerable amount of . . .

. . . picking in the fields, putting the berries directly into pint-sized baskets. From the fields, these are taken to adjacent sheds where they are crated both for quick freezing and for immediate shipment. One of the most important quick freezing plants in the country is located at Ponchatoula, four miles from Hammond; its owner, Marion T. Fannally, has been a pioneer in developing and expanding the process which has made fresh frozen strawberries available the year round; he now absorbs a large part of the crop remaining after the famous auctions, which take place in a small log cabin near the station, are over for the year. The lion's share of the early crop is shipped out, via the special train appropriately called the "Crimson Flyer," via . . .

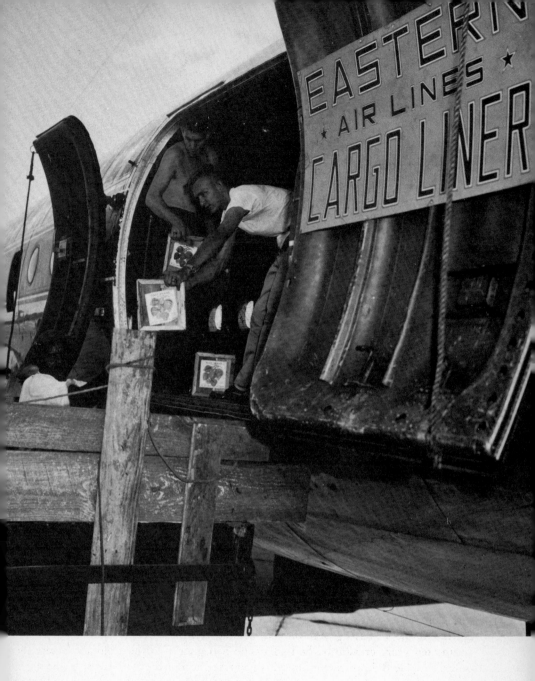

. . . refrigerated trucks and via airplane to markets all over the United States. Airplane shipment permits the delivery of fresh berries to the Northern markets within ten hours of picking time, and berries thus shipped naturally command a higher price than those which take longer in transit. Moreover, the type of transport plane used can carry more crates than a refrigerated freight car. Under these circumstances, it is hardly surprising that air service is in greater and greater demand all the time; as many as four laden planes sometimes go out from the Strawberry Capital of Hammond in a single day.

"HERE COMES JACK"

To me, the young springtime vendors provide one of the most attractive features on the Airline; as its name implies it is designed to facilitate speed over the shortest possible route between two important points, not to tempt a leisurely wanderer to linger amid scenes of natural beauty. Like most people, we travel over it largely to save time and do not feel disappointed if it offers few distractions. However, this does not mean that a diversion is unwelcome and recently an unusual one was offered us by a strange nomad, who proclaimed himself by a sign reading, "Here Comes Jack."

We caught a fleeting glimpse of him as we were hurrying toward Baton Rouge and were so intrigued by the sight of his queer wagon, drawn by three burros, one with a goat on its back, that we swung around and stopped. A closer view only increased our amazed interest. Elemore Morgan descended from the car in which we were riding and asked if he might take some pictures. The nomad graciously consented and, the ice having been broken, willingly engaged in conversation.

Some ten years previously, he told us, he had gone into the Colorado desert for his health. (He did not reveal how this happened to fail him, or anything about his previous history, and we did not feel we should pry into these matters.) In the desert he acquired the burros to carry his camping equipment; then he decided it would be still easier to move this about if he had a wagon too. He next added goats, to insure a milk supply, chickens to insure eggs and a dog for company. Then he decided that he was ready to travel. He figured he could cover his expenses by selling picture postcards of himself.

His trip took him first south to Mexico and then north to Canada. Next he decided that he would like to participate in a Mardi Gras celebration, so he headed for New Orleans. He reached it without difficulty, but there he met his first great disappointment: the authorities declined to let him appear in a parade without a special permit,

for which they proposed to charge fifty dollars. This unreasonable demand roused his wrath and he shook the dust of New Orleans from his feet. He was now headed for the Atlantic Ocean, which he intended to enrich with a rock pried loose from the mountains of Colorado. After he had tossed this into the briny deep, he was going back to the desert. He had no idea of leaving it again. Not that his plan of self-support had been unsuccessful; he had sold any number of picture postcards. But he had found Kansas too dusty, Louisiana too muggy and most places generally inferior to his chosen habitation.

Having unburdened himself of this saga, our nomad began to show signs of weariness and announced his intention of bedding down for the night by the roadside. We did not wish to intrude upon his privacy, so we took our leave, after Elemore had assured him that Jack was not the only man who had ever been disappointed in Carnival. Then we resumed our journey, regretfully conscious that we should probably never look on his like again.

However, the Airline does offer a more dependable diversion in the form of . . .

195

DESCENDANTS OF DINOSAURS

. . . the fishermen who perennially angle for choupiques in the marshes along the edges of the road. (There is no lack of these marshes, for the Airline was built straight across a raw swamp.) The anglers are nearly always Negroes, for colored people are more appreciative of the choupiques' merits than most white folks; they use long poles, large lines and big hooks to capture their prey. This is an extraordinary creature, the single living member of an entire order of fish, whose family history goes back to the age of the dinosaur. Because of a rudimentary lung, it is able to live in mud as well as water, and its jaws are set with sharp teeth, which are a menace . . .

. . . to an unwary fisherman. (The wise angler carries a pair of pliers to remove the hook from the choupique's mouth.) But it offers good sport, for it is extremely game and it also provides plentiful eating; it is not infrequently as much as three feet long. Prior to cooking, it is sometimes soaked overnight in oil and vinegar to give it the substance which it lacks in its natural state; but it is generally eaten smoked, and the fishermen, on their return home, give it their best attention. Meanwhile, a cup of coffee or a can of beer would be very refreshing after a day in the broiling sun. Fortunately, there are cafés and bars as well as marshes along the Airline and segregation works both ways.

MY OWN FAVORITE STOPPING PLACE IS ROUSSEL'S

My favorite stopping place on the Airline is Roussel's Restaurant at LaPlace. Outside, it is wholly unremarkable and, as far as that goes, there is nothing about its appearance inside to set it apart from dozens of other roadside restaurants in Louisiana. A lunch counter runs along the side facing the entrance with a bar adjoining it at a right angle. Small square tables with marbleized tops are scattered over about half the floor space; the other half is pre-empted by juke boxes and slot machines. The most crowded part of the establishment is generally the bar, but the slot machines come next in popularity. The clatter of coins resounds above all the other noises in the restaurant and it is by no means a quiet place. A juke box is almost always in operation. The patrons and the personnel are on terms of hail-fellow-well-met with each other. The front door bangs constantly. All in all, it is a far cry from the typical tea shoppe, adorned with neat little bunches of flowers and Godey prints, which, in many other parts of the country, is apt to be the traveler's best bet outside metropolitan areas. That, however, is not one of the reasons I like it so much. I will try to explain what some of these reasons are.

1. It has the neatest and most attentive waitresses of any roadside restaurant in Louisiana with which I am familiar. I have never seen one of these girls when her white uniform was not spotless or when her face was not wreathed in smiles. And the service is equally prompt and pleasant whether you order a solitary cup of coffee or a full-course meal for a party of six.

2. It serves the best old-fashioneds of any roadside restaurant in Louisiana with which I am familiar. Felix, the bartender, is justly famous for these and, if you have been motoring most of the day and are still thirty miles from your destination, a good old-fashioned can make all the difference in the frame of mind with which you face the final stretch of road and New Orleans traffic.

3. It has the best food of any roadside restaurant in Louisiana with which I am familiar. The only difficulty lies in choosing between such dishes as turtle soup, Creole gumbo and crayfish bisque. And then there is the further handicap of knowing that when you have finished with one of these, you will not have room left for fried chicken.

4. It has the most attractive proprietress of any roadside restaurant in Louisiana with which I am familiar. Mrs. Roussel has short, curly gray hair, rosy cheeks, a pleasingly plump figure and a manner which is at one and the same time forthright, cordial and composed—a difficult combination for any woman to achieve, let alone one who runs an establishment like this in addition to a home where her grandchildren range at will and her friends are always welcome. The only thing that seems to upset her is the sign of hesitation on the part of a visitor to presume overmuch on her boundless hospitality.

"You really mean you can't stop any longer today? Fresh coffee's dripping right now and we've got a dozen bottles of nice cold beer on the ice. Well then, the next time. Just wait till I tell you what I've got packed away in the deep freeze. If you weren't in such a hurry, I'd like to show you."

The next time the visit probably will be longer. But it was by no means brief the last time. It couldn't be. I like both the restaurant and Mrs. Roussel too much.

THE STRETCH BETWEEN NEW IBERIA AND
JEANERETTE IS THE MOST BEAUTIFUL

AND THE PARABLE OF THE WISE AND UNWISE
VIRGINS IS ENACTED HERE

One of the loveliest stretches of country road in Louisiana, to my way of thinking, is the one between Jeanerette and New Iberia—and this applies both to the "pave" on one side of Bayou Teche and to the stretch of gravel on the other. They are shaded by magnificent trees which, even in midsummer, give an illusion of coolness; and from the highway the trees stretch back toward the bayou in beautiful groves. Some of these groves have an open, sunny look; they surround well-kept houses, fronted by smooth lawns. Others are dense and dim; only ruins remain of the homes they once sheltered. But they are still abiding places of mystery and romance.

Midway down the gravel stretch is a Negro meeting house known as Little Zorah Missionary Baptist Church, which serves not only as a place of worship, but as a civic center for the Negro community. Its pastor, known by his people as the "Rev," encourages them to produce plays based on Bible stories. One of these plays, which tells the story of the wise and foolish virgins, was so successful when it was originally produced that it is now repeated every year. It is given during the last dark moon of May and is called "The Candle Drill."

The Reverend and his Elders meet the participants in this pageant near the four corners in front of a shoe repair shop, about a mile down the bayou from the church. Here the procession is formed. A "bride" and "groom" lead off, followed by the "wise virgins" wearing white headdresses and carrying lighted candles. Next come the "foolish virgins," carrying unlighted candles and wearing colored headdresses. All other church members form in the rear.

They march briskly along through the twilight, their soft voices filling the air with melody as they sing, "Meeting at the Old Camp Grounds Tonight." When they reach the churchyard the air changes to "When the Bridegroom Cometh." They are walking more slowly now; the grass makes a rustling sound as they shuffle through it, circling the church three times before they enter.

It is a bare little building, lighted by coal oil lamps. The men hang their hats on nails around the wall. The Reverend and the Elders seat themselves on the platform behind the pulpit; then the "bride" and "groom" take their places before this, flanked on either side by the "virgins." The Reverend performs a ceremony, symbolizing the marriage of Christ and the Church. Then he orders the "groom" to

salute the "bride," and, momentarily, the solemnity of the occasion gives way to merriment. But soon a more reverent note is sounded again; the Reverend reads the parable on which the pageant is founded and leads his congregation in earnest prayer. Then he turns the program over to his master of ceremonies and song and verse become the order of the day.

A tall, slim Negro with a deep bass voice leads off with, "The Old Rugged Cross." By the time he has proclaimed that he will change the cross for a crown, the coal oil lamps are smoking badly. Chimeda White, one of the "wise virgins," inquires tunefully, "Are You Washed in the Blood?" Zenobia Villeto, a visitor from a neighboring church, renders, "I Got Religion and I Can't Sit Down." But no one seems startled or curious as a result, though one small boy suffers from stage fright and forgets his lines in the middle of his piece. Another, blissfully drowsy with the heat, finally drifts off to sleep. But most of the children are contentedly preoccupied with all-day suckers. The real hit of the evening comes when Elva Lee Rogers, wearing a bright silk dress and a ribbon in her hair, recites, with a deadpan face:

> "Listen what's all that I been saying?
>   What on earth took charge of me?
> When that music coming now?
>   Driving my 'liggion up a tree
> Clear out that fiddle
>   Don't you try that trick again
> You don't know I could be tempted
>   But you like to make me sin."

The program comes to a close with a prayer and a song in which everyone joins, while the Elders take up the offering. There are no refreshments afterwards. "If any man hunger—let him eat at home!" advises the Reverend. This parody of the Master's words holds no conscious irreverence. Like everything else about the pageant, it is in harmony with the very essence of the Negro congregation's faith in God.

THE STRETCH BETWEEN VACHERIE AND DONALDSONVILLE CLARIFIES THE MEANING OF MIRACLES

THROUGH THE CELEBRATION OF ST. AMICO'S FEAST DAY

If the happy wanderer is free to roam the Sunday after Easter, he should certainly choose the stretch of River Road between Vacherie and Donaldsonville. For this is the day that the statue of St. Amico emerges from the small chapel of galvanized iron which is its sanctuary and makes its triumphal progress to the Church of the Ascension in Donaldsonville.

There is a touching story to account for the veneration in which the humble and holy man is held in this locality: an Italian workman, Tony Musco, was hurrying home one evening, desperately worried about his little son, Lucien, who lay grievously ill. On his way the distraught father was stopped by a stranger, who asked for a night's lodging. Tony did not have much to offer, he said; just a shakedown in the same room with a sick child. But if such poor comfort would suffice. . . . The stranger accepted, simply and gratefully. On his arrival at the Muscos' modest dwelling, he took the small sufferer from the crib and held him close. Somewhat later, the stranger suggested that Lucien should be given food and, to the amazement of his parents, he ate and seemed to relish it. In the morning, the mysterious visitor was gone, his identity still undisclosed. But Lucien, well on the road to recovery, pointed to a crude print of St. Amico in a corner, and inquired, "Isn't that the kind man who stayed with us last night?"

Since then the Muscos have never doubted that they had entertained a man of God unawares. They saved their money and built a small shrine. Additional cures in the neighborhood and many votive offerings indicated its enlargement. The community helped to build the new chapel and raised the money to import a more impressive statue from Italy. Now young and old join in the procession which begins at the door of the shrine and . . .

. . . proceeds along the River Road. The levee is its loveliest at this season, white with clover, bordered by cream-colored thistle blossoms and pink "buttercups." Cattle and horses and sheep are all grazing peacefully upon it. The road may still be wet with recent rain, but the marchers do not mind. The air is fresh and fragrant, the day is worthy of their saint. They parade with spirit.

The cross-bearer comes first, flanked by two flag-bearers. Then, on his float, comes St. Amico, wearing over his scarlet robes the silk stole, reserved for festive occasions, to which are attached the medals and ornaments bestowed on him as thank offerings. Next comes the colored band, zestfully playing, "America the Beautiful." A second, smaller float follows, on which statues of the Virgin Mary and St. Joseph are mounted. This small float is carried by girls and women. Two of the little girls delay the procession to wipe off the images with clean cloths. Everything must be done decently and in order.

The quiet cattle turn to look at the procession as it passes, then calmly resume their grazing. Clusters of Negroes, loitering in front of roadside cabins, stare at the statues, and occasionally there is a stifled laugh. The band has run out of patriotic tunes and has begun to play jazz. But the wanderer knows that St. Amico would understand and love these people, just as they understand and love him.

Some of the women in the procession are dragging small, reluctant children after them. One of them is nursing her baby. The men in the procession are mopping their faces and voicing their discomfort in terms which are not, strictly speaking, devout. Never mind. As I said before, St. Amico would understand these people and make allowances.

At last the marchers reach their destination. The floats and the worshippers disappear inside the Church of the Ascension. But the members of the colored band . . .

. . . hang their instruments on the branches of the great trees outside the church and, leaving some small boys to watch over their drums and trombones, go away to drink beer.

They know they will not need to hurry over this refreshment. It will be a long time before High Mass is over and St. Amico is ready to leave the central aisle of the church. The pile of crisp bills and printed slips surrounding him on his float grows higher and higher. And still devotees keep leaving their seats to bring further petitions: dollar bills clipped to form prayers, notes scrawled on scraps of paper. No one doubts that St. Amico reads both kinds with equal ease.

It will not be surprising if the happy wanderer adds his petition to the others. He may do so almost instinctively, because he has become part of a mass movement; but it is doubtful if he will do so derisively. For the first time has been made manifest to him the meaning of miracles.

THE STRETCH BETWEEN LAFAYETTE AND
CROWLEY IS THE ONE I TRAVEL MOST NOWADAYS

DRAB WINTER PRECEDES DAZZLING SPRING IN THE RICE FIELDS

Lately the stretch of road I have traveled over most frequently is the highway between Crowley and Lafayette. This takes me through the town of Rayne, which specializes in frogs' legs, and the town of Scott, which specializes in buggies, and the village of Duson, which is named for the founders of Crowley. Otherwise, there are just a few scattered buildings. And it is all very flat, with only one small bridge arching above the level land and, against the skyline, mounds of straw left over from threshing. I miss mountains in Louisiana, which is natural for a woman whose heritage includes both Vermont and Virginia. Nevertheless, this flat stretch of road has come to seem very beautiful to me. For on either side of it, as far as the eye can see, are the rice fields.

In winter, these fields are dun-colored, and they might be drab, were it not for the serpentine levees, highlighted by pockets of water, which curve along the dormant land. These rice levees must not be confused with the river levees. The former are low lying, rising only a foot or so above the areas which they control. But they have an exquisite symmetry; and their elevation, slight as it is, redeems the fields from monotony. Cattle remain on the land throughout the winter; in good weather, they range over the stubble, feeding contentedly upon it; in bad weather, they huddle against the stacks, nibbling at the old straw in a gingerly way. Families of "muley" ducks are also there, indifferent to the weather; they make no sound, as they gather in clusters about the small pools which the levees entrap. Both the ducks and the pools seem to take their color from the sky—blue on a bright day, white on a day when the clouds close in. But whether blue or white, the pools shine like mirrors and the plumage of the ducks gleams. It is this dazzling quality of theirs that gives sparkle to the wintry landscape.

Then, in the spring, the land is prepared for early planting by "busting" the levees—

that is to say, by opening them up and laying them flat; then it is disced and harrowed and leveled to a firm, even seed bed. The actual seeding is done either by planes or with a tractor-drawn drill which has two compartments, one for seed rice and one for fertilizer. During the leveling process, clouds of dust follow the seeding machine. When the planting is finished, the land is no longer either drab or dormant; its color has changed to a warm brown; it is vitalized through its impregnation. Only those who have never intimately known seedtime and harvest are so blind as to believe that the visible signs which promise fertility are confined to the animal kingdom.

All the land is not planted simultaneously; the process is progressive. If a man has a thousand acres, he spaces his seeding to balance with his harvesting. Naturally, the early varieties of rice are planted first; then come those which mature later. Thus the fields are ripening and ready for harvesting on a continuous run. The levees are constructed to control the flow of the irrigation waters and their depth. And presently . . .

LAGNIAPPE CROPS

. . . the young plants begin to show above the water—jade green at first, when they are slim and delicate, emerald green later on, when they are stouter and sturdier. Under normal conditions, the gentle rains and the balmy sunshine of spring have germinated the seed, and the farmer has been praying for a happy combination of these. If his prayers have gone unanswered, he has flooded his fields through irrigagation and drained them off again. In either case, by mid-May the fields are green.

During this period, the levees have been carefully maintained: patched, repaired, built up, to keep the water at its proper depth. Their serpentine form is not accidental nor is it the result of an eye for symmetry; the "Contour" or "Crooked Levee" system is the one which advantageously follows the slight variations of land elevation. It requires less water than the old "Straight Levee" system and it keeps the water at more even depth. The cost of a "Contour Levee" system, in most instances, pays for its installation within a year, partly through a saving on water costs, partly through better weed and insect control and partly through increase of yield in the crop.

By June, the traveler along the highway sees that the irrigation ditches, which were empty during the winter, except when intermittently supplied with rain, are now full to overflowing. He sees too that the growth of the crop is so rapid that he can notice a difference in it from week to week, almost from day to day. When the plants are about a foot above the water—that is, tall enough to shelter from predatory birds—he also notices his old friends the "muley" ducks again. But the number of these has greatly increased. Spring, as we have remarked before, is the season of fertility. So now, dozens and dozens of baby ducks have been turned into the irrigated rice fields, which offer them a natural habitat. The thrifty farmers who are responsible for their presence are intent on raising not only one crop, but two: by the time the rice is ready to harvest, the ducks are ready to market.

There is also another lagniappe crop: this consists of crayfish in such abundance that the farmer or his enterprising offspring has only to place an open sack at a levee cutoff and, with breath-taking rapidity, it will be filled. He can repeat this process over and over again, assuring himself, his family and his neighbors of all the crayfish bisque they can devour for days to come.

When the rice is headed . . .

IN THESE RADIANT FIELDS

... the highway has become a mere channel through the tall, golden grain, swaying in the breeze. It is waist-high and it has the same density as wheat.

In these radiant fields the omnipresent rice birds may have done some damage by milking the young grain before the dough stage; or the "Blue Peter"—a species of gallinule—may have destroyed all the plants in his nesting area, which can be a ten-foot square. But after all, the crop has few enemies and its abundance seldom fails.

By the time the grain is waist-high, the water has already been "turned off" and the land given time to solidify. If it were not well drained, low pockets of standing water would hinder harvesting and reduce the yield per acre. When the land is ready to support heavy equipment, the rice may be harvested by either one of two methods, each of which has its advocates. The older method consists of using a binder to cut the rice and tie it into bundles; then to put these bundles into shocks and allow them to dry; afterward hauling ...

. . . them by wagon or truck to the threshing machine.

The more modern method consists of adapting the standard wheat combines to rice field conditions by equipping them with "cat tracks" or large "doughnut" rubber tires. From the combine the rice is hauled to a dryer, where the moisture content is reduced to a safe level. Then the dried rice is stored or milled.

Whichever method has been used, harvesting is over by mid-October. The fields which the traveler sees are still golden; but the gold is like a carpet now and the road has become part of the pattern again. For the last time this year, he has noticed . . .

WHAT HAPPENS TO ROUGH RICE

... the straw blown from a threshing machine into a stack and the rough rice conveyed to the bed of a tight-bodied truck. The stack remains in the field, to become one of those mounds which rise perpetually against the skyline; the truck will almost immediately be on its way to a mill. And the traveler may follow it there if he chooses, for there are many mills along this stretch of road and visitors are welcome.

The first stop is logically near the unloading platform. The custom of using sacks in the fields to receive the newly threshed rice is not as widespread as it used to be. More often, the sacks are piled just inside the unloading platform; and awaiting the arrival of the truck is sure to be . . .

. . . a Negro, who will help unload the rice and get it into sacks for milling.

The first milling operation consists of running the rough rice over monitors, clippers and shakers, which remove foreign material. At this stage the rice has been thoroughly cleaned, but still retains its outer husk. Next, it goes through a so-called "stone," which hulls it. The third operation is the removal of the outer cuticle on the grain of the rice itself, which is known as the rice bran; this is done by so-called "hullers." The final step in milling is the removal of rice polish which lies immediately adjacent to the grain itself. This is done by a piece of machinery known as a "brush" and the product which is obtained is called rice polish.

I have been much intrigued to discover that . . .

... in the rice-milling business, a "stone" is not a stone, but a mixture of cement, carborundum and brine. A "huller" is not really a huller because the hull has already been removed. A "brush" is not really a brush; it consists of leather strips applied to a wooden drum and friction is produced by the pressure of this revolving drum against a wire screen. Practically every piece of machinery used in a rice mill is an adaptation of machinery used in processing wheat, coffee and cocoa.

After the rice has been milled, it is known as "clean" rice, and is usually packed in "pockets," a pocket being one hundred pounds of rice. The operator receives the rice from an automatic weighing and dumping machine which has been filled from above. He closes the pocket with an electric sewing machine and shoves it onto a truck, from which it is later unloaded for repackaging into containers or for storage.

The rice fields which the traveler observes from the road fulfill the Biblical prophecy that seedtime and harvest shall never vanish from the earth; as I have said before, their crops have few enemies and their abundance never fails from year to year. Based upon their continuing yield and sharing ...

DOMINOES AND DESTINY

. . . their perennial quality is the game of dominoes, which began farther back than any one can remember and which is still going on. The local headquarters of the American Rice Growers' Cooperative Association provides the setting for it; the players are the rice farmers, the rice brokers, the rough-rice buyers and the operators of the rice mills—in short, all the men whose business logically brings them to the "Co-op." The owners of the rice mills encourage these representatives of theirs to go there, for the sake of the information they can obtain, both directly and indirectly. This process requires experience, but it is apparently a very jovial, almost a casual one. In the midst of a game, one player may remark to another, after a certain amount of horseplay, that he has not been in the market lately; his adversary will very probably reply, "Oh, yeah?" secure in the knowledge that he has concluded a very satisfactory purchase just before coming to the "Co-op" and that news of this has not yet had time to leak out. Another player, apparently completely absorbed in dominoes, may suddenly rise, saunter over to the rough-rice table and buy out the entire line, involving the expenditure of more than a hundred thousand dollars. As one man leaves the game, another immediately takes his place, and there is always a group of onlookers, who are well aware that the low stakes for which the domino game is played bear no relation to the very high ones that are actually involved.

AND LOGICALLY LEADS TO THE RICE FESTIVAL

"PLEASURING OURSELVES" AT THE RICE
CARNIVAL

"When the crop is in the field it belongs to the Lord; when it is in the warehouse it is yours."

Thus runs a time-honored saying of the region. And though it is a region which puts its trust in the Lord to a greater degree than many others, it does not start to celebrate until the harvest is in. Then Crowley holds its annual Rice Festival.

This is a spontaneous celebration, locally sponsored, locally staged. Several days before the actual festival, Parkerson Avenue, which forms its setting, begins to take on a gala air from the station to the courthouse. Pennants float from wires suspended across the street, pillars are wrapped in bunting and shop windows feature the multitudinous uses and benefits of rice in so original and lavish a way that it is evident merchants have vied with each other to enlighten, attract and satisfy the public. The response to this effort is tremendous; the sidewalks are crowded with people who . . .

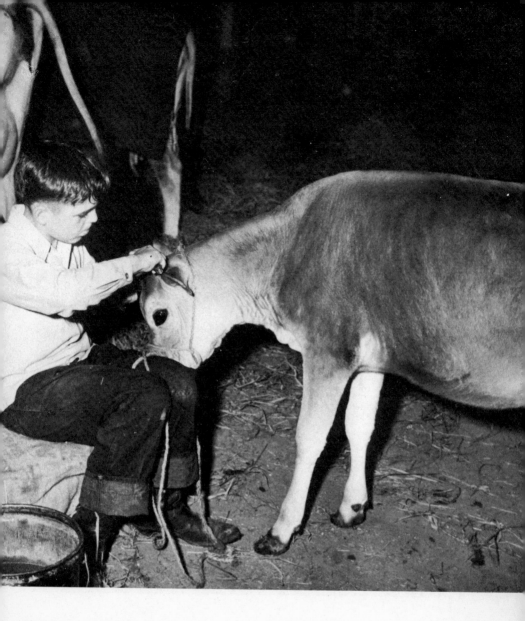

. . . have come to "pleasure themselves." Strangers and sightseers have not yet arrived, in any considerable numbers; these first-comers are the men who raise and market the rice, accompanied by their families or their sweethearts. This is their own special holiday, their interval of relaxation between periods of hard work, their opportunity to observe, appraise and enjoy the displays prepared for them. Their mood is very different from that of Carnival crowds—less boisterous, less devil-may-care, more conscious of the underlying meaning of the celebration.

On the eve of the festival everything is in readiness for it to begin. At the station end of the avenue is an agricultural show, comprising not only cattle, but swine and poultry, farm products and farm machinery. Men have brought their prize stock, women their best preserves, children their pet calves. The region abounds in fine herds and plentiful fruits and there is no lack from which to choose.

A little farther on . . .

ACADIAN ARTS AND CRAFTS

... the reproduction of a typical, primitive Acadian house is the center of attraction. It is made of wood, with wooden shutters at the windows, a spacious mud chimney and a split-shingle roof. Its two rooms are connected by a covered passage. But standard furnishings have been eliminated in order to make room for examples of palmetto work and other forms of handicraft. An immense loom, operated by Mrs. Ambroise LeBlanc, who wears an authentic Acadian dress, dominates the larger room.

All the wares are supervised by Louise Olivier of Arnaudville, who first visualized the possibilities of Acadian craft and then turned them to practical account. No wonder that "Miss Lulu's" greetings to her visitors at the Acadian house are permeated with pride as well as pleasure!

The sightseers are now in a mood for lighter amusement. This is supplied by ...

THE FROG JUMPING CONTEST IS ALSO A LEG SHOW

. . . the frog jumping contest. The participants in this contest are girls, dressed in shorts, who have possessed themselves of bullfrogs, drawn from the plentiful local supply. One by one, the girls, carrying their frogs, are shepherded toward platform scales, in charge of an official weigher. After they have been weighed, they line up at a "jumping box" that has a rice sack attached to it, on which the frogs can get a grip. In turn, the contestants place their frogs on this box, which is literally their jumping-off place. Some of them, willingly take the plunge; others, require prodding from the rear. But sooner or later each jumps into space and the one which covers the most ground is the winner. The crowd closes in, laughing uproariously and egging the contestants to a finish. Eventually, in the midst of loud cheers, the race is completed.

From the picturesque and the hilarious, we go on to the glamorous and the symbolic. In front of the Egan Hotel an immense platform has been erected and here . . .

A SHEAF OF RICE FOR A SCEPTRE

. . . the Queens are chosen and crowned. There are two—the Children's Queen and the International Rice Queen. Both are selected on the spot by judges who scrutinize, with meticulous care, first the children and then the young girls who, one by one, mount the platform where they are greeted by the Queens of the previous year, who take them by the hand, lead them about, and finally assign them to a place in a charmed and charming circle. (Never shall I forget the complete poise, the engaging winsomeness, with which Claude Lyons, aged seven, who was the Child Queen of '46, received the child candidates of '47.) After a brief consultation on the part of the judges, the least promising candidates are eliminated; then, after more deliberation, a second group. This process continues until only two or three are left out of the original twenty or thirty. (When Mary Alice Toso, representing Venezuela, won the coveted honor at the first International Rice Festival, the deliberations went on and on; though her grace and beauty indubitably entitled her to first place, there were several close contenders.) At last the final choice is made. Then the outstanding citizen to whom the Festival has been "dedicated" as one who is entitled to special recognition, because of his contribution to rice culture, places the crown of gilded rice on the new Queen's head and gives her the spray of rice which serves as her

sceptre. Later in the day she rides on a float, to receive the tribute of the crowds which have now swelled to tens of thousands and, in the evening, she presides at a grand ball. But her reign begins, then and there, on the central platform.

In some ways the Rice Festival at Crowley seems to me the most significant of all the local celebrations with which I am familiar. Perhaps this is partly because the culture of rice is so supremely beautiful, from the time the wet fields are overspread with green shoots to the time the golden stalks are top-heavy with grain. Perhaps it is partly because this Festival of the Deep South comes close on the calendar to the date of national Thanksgiving, instituted by the Pilgrims, which, all my life, has been associated with a happy harvest. But, most of all, I think it is because rice has a universal meaning and fulfills a universal need. If I am not mistaken, no one other staple, except wheat, represents the fundamental food of so many millions. The celebration in Crowley is not merely a matter of local pride; it is a symbol of kinship with every other rice-producing region in the world, a pledge of co-operation from Louisianians in the great task of feeding their fellow creatures.

Section Three

FIELDS AND·MARSHES

FIELD TRIALS

LATE JANUARY is bobwhite time in Louisiana; and, in the rolling hill-lands of the Feliciana Parishes, which lie between St. Francisville and Clinton, it is also "Field Trial Time."

The narrow, sandy roads wind in and out of the fields covered with dusty pink sage, which fades into the dark green background of the piney woods. The bright red berries on the yaupon trees which form the hedgerows glisten against the blue-white winter sky. The entire area is a happy hunting ground for both dog and man.

From most of the southern states bird dog men have been driving for long hours to get to the Southeastern Regional Meet in time for the drawing of lots which place their dogs in the trials. Some of the travelers have expensive outfits—trailers for their dogs, handlers, feed and equipment; others . . .

... just put their dogs in the back seat of an old jalopy, already crowded by members of the family, and come right on. Both groups know that any man, woman or child who thrills at the sight of a good bird dog frozen on a point is sure of a royal welcome at headquarters; both also know that the dogs crowded into the jalopies are just as likely to win the championship cups and ribbons, awarded at the end of the trials, as the dogs who came in the trailers.

Preparations for the trials have been going on for days. The courses have been marked, the coveys of birds located, and saddle horses for the "gallery" provided, often up to the number of one hundred and fifty. By dawn of the first day, headquarters cabin is a beehive of activity, for nine miles of course must be worked over before noon. When the dog wagon is loaded with pointers and setters and the judges are assembled, everyone is ready to go.

The flight (i.e., pair of dogs), held by their handlers, is on the starting line, awaiting the signal, tense with excitement. This tension is contagious; it runs through the gallery of horsemen. The expectant silence is broken only by a smothered cough, by the snap of a cigarette lighter, by the creak of a saddle. Then suddenly the dogs are off, the horses break ranks, everyone talks at once as the group surges forward, crowding the judges and handlers, eager to see the first point. Necessarily, the gallery is held back to give the dogs freedom to work from cover to cover; but it has spread out, forming into separate parties, some riding along the hedgerows and some along the dikes which border the stock ponds.

A good dog wastes little time going over unlikely spots. He heads straight for the likeliest bird cover. The intensity with which he changes from flashing speed to graven immobility is pure drama. His handler, jubilant, raises his hand or waves his hat and cries, "Point, judges!" The officials ride up, followed by the gallery. By this time the handler has dismounted, and is standing quietly beside his dog, waiting for the official signal. "Show your game," directs the presiding judge.

The handler walks in the direction along which his dog's nose is all but riveted. A dozen feathered projectiles are catapulted from beneath his feet with drumming beat of frantic wings. The handler draws a pistol and fires a blank cartridge. (No game is bagged at a field trial.) The dog has not moved. He is "steady to wing and to shot." The judges nod approvingly, and a whisper of approbation runs through the gallery. The birds, now in full flight, head for distant cover. Not until he receives the awaited word does the dog leap away in search for the next find.

Frequently an outstanding dog commands an immediate offer from one enthusiast to another. For instance, the pointer, Milo, found four coveys in twenty minutes during the course of a recent trial. Directly afterward, his master, who was doing the handling himself, was approached by one of the horsemen in the gallery with an extravagant bid. The owner laughed it off; there was not enough money in the world to buy Milo, he said conclusively. Sometimes, however, there is trading with mutually satisfactory results, though the cups and ribbons still mean more than any cash returns.

Even before the horses were fed and saddled and the dog wagon loaded at day-break, a coffee pot was bubbling on the stove and the barbecue of a beef had begun. The hunters gulp down early morning coffee before starting over the course; but by noon they are ready for more and they are thankful to know that, during their absence, the coffee pot has been refilled. They are ravenously hungry too, and long before they are back at camp, the pungent aroma of the barbecue assails their nostrils. By the time they reach headquarters, it is done to a turn. They file past a long table, where they are supplied with paper plates, paper cups and cutlery. Then they

230

are served coffee again, and with it a hearty meal—thick slices of bread, heaping portions of potato salad, chunks of barbecued meat covered with rich sauce. At the end of the table stands a big barrel, equipped with a spigot; the hunter takes a second paper cup and helps himself to water. After this has been consumed, like as not, the diner returns to the head of the table and, without waiting for service this time, helps himself to more coffee, more bread, more potato salad, more barbe-cued meat, more rich sauce. When he has eaten his fill, he sets out again for the field.

This time the going is harder. The cold frosty air has mellowed to midday warmth. The sunny atmosphere, in itself, is conducive to drowsiness; when a man is replete with hearty food, he finds this drowsiness doubly difficult to combat. His horse is tired, and its saddle has grown harder since morning. The gallery is less alert. The judges and handlers are still vigilant because they must watch a fresh flight; however, it is duty rather than delight which keeps them so now. No one is ill-tempered and there is no sense of strain; but there has been a letdown.

By five o'clock the sun has lost its mellowness and is low on the horizon. By six the Southland's brief twilight has become "good dark." It is growing cold. The ride back to camp is slow and silent. The cheering glass that awaits the weary sportsman at headquarters is more than welcome. For a brief period the day's events are the topic of absorbed discussion. Then the crowd disperses to near-by plantations and villages for a night's rest before a second day of trials. The dogs are tired too. They take their rest like the others.

WILD GEESE

If the wanderer in Louisiana is by nature a sportsman, he will find, throughout October, that the kindred spirits with whom he is associated are alerted, by the barking of their dogs, to the sound of honking geese. The migration has begun on the Mississippi Flyway.

This flyway consists of several different migrations. The first to come into Louisiana are the Blue Geese, with an occasional Snow Goose gleaming among them. Often they circle over New Orleans, apparently either confused or attracted by the lights of the Crescent City; and all the time they are circling they are also calling. This call is entirely different from that of the Canada Geese, who follow along afterward; it is more of a yelp and less of a honk. After the yelping has ceased, the sportsman is conscious of a strange lack in the sounds of the city. But it does not depress him. The note has been sounded which presages the time for which he has long waited. He knows that he too will soon be on his way to the mouth of the river.

The Canada Geese, in V-formations, are led by wise old ganders, who have flown many times from the nesting grounds in the wilds of Northern Canada to the wintering places in the marshes of South Louisiana. These leaders know that the passage is fraught with danger from inclement weather and hunters' guns; but, to a surprising degree, they keep their followers safe.

As they near their destination, the leader's enthusiasm intensifies; he increases his flight speed and urges his followers on with loud, raucous calls. They answer him, honking somewhat less vociferously than he does; but none of them lags behind. The flight is a high one; it can be watched by day, but it can seldom be seen by night, even when the moon is full; the sound, rather than the sight, proclaims its approach.

Its arrival marks the beginning of winter as this term is understood in Louisiana: cool crisp weather, with a nip in the evening and morning air, but with abundant sunshine and mellow warmth at noon. It also marks an exodus from their homes of a large proportion of the male population, which takes to camps in the fields, swamps and marshes. Nowhere else that I know of does hunting in all its phases become so absorbing a preoccupation.

The sportsmen, with their guides, go by pirogue to the blinds in the marshes, where the guides call . . . .

... the geese into gun range. The kill is allowed to lie where it falls until the limit has been reached; then the day's bag is gathered up and the hunter returns to his camp. A hunter of average ability has every reason to hope that he can get his limit between the prescribed period of half an hour before sunrise till half an hour before sunset.

It sometimes happens, however, here as elsewhere, that a wounded bird escapes, and Elemore Morgan tells the following story of some which he photographed: two Canada Geese suddenly dropped into a pond which was the habitat of domestic geese and ducks. The owner of these, Mrs. Braeme, welcomed the newcomers, fed and gentled them; they stayed on, using the pond as headquarters, but absenting themselves to take a flight over a near-by swamp area every day; toward sundown when Mrs. Braeme honked the horn of her automobile to signify that supper time was approaching, they always promptly returned.

236

Eventually the gander was killed by a hunter, while the pair was out on one of its daily flights. The goose was wounded, but managed to return to the pond, where she has remained ever since, faithful to the memory of her consort. Other suitors have approached her, but she is not interested. Geese mate for life.

BIRD CITY

Whatever the geography books say, an island is not always "a small body of land surrounded by water." At several points along the southern sea-rim of Louisiana, great subterranean deposits of salt were forced upward, in bygone ages, by the terrific pressures of geologic deposits above them; and wherever this occurred, the upward gush of salt lifted some surface soil above the surrounding marshland to form isolated knolls of high ground. One of these came into the possession of the Avery family more than a century ago, and that is Avery Island, whose salt mine, pepper sauce factory, oil fields, jungle gardens, bamboo groves and bird sanctuary have given it world-wide renown.

Try to envision a plug of pure rock salt, five miles deep and eight miles in circumference, covered with a blanket of topsoil whose general contour is not unlike that of a quilt draped over a bushel basket. The soil above that mammoth salt-plug grows the hottest red peppers known to man. They are the source of the Tabasco Sauce that is manufactured there in a great factory whose brick walls are encased in fig vines. Two or three miles beyond it, another tall factory-like building bestrides the entrance of a vertical shaft that leads down to the mine whose chambered compartments are floored, walled and roofed with gleaming, crystalline salt while eighty-foot columns of the same material provide a supporting structure.

Above ground are not only the pepper fields and the oil fields, but gardens in which plants from all the world luxuriate. There are irises from Siberia, Spain and Kyushu; a forest of timber bamboo from Ceylon; wisterias from the antipodes; podocarps from Tibet; taro plants from Hawaii; lotus from the Nile. These were all brought there by the late head of the Avery Island dynasty, Edward Avery McIlhenny— M'sieu Ned to the surrounding countryside.

As a youth he led expeditions into the Arctic. A dictionary of Eskimo dialects he compiled is still a standard work of reference. He frequently wrestled great alligators for the sheer sport of it. His life history of the alligator is one of the few definitive treatises on the subject. In his big-game hunting, he regarded it as unsportsmanlike to bag bear with any other weapon than a great knife. And, among other things, single-handed, he saved the snowy egret from extinction, which brings us to . . .

238

. . . Bird City.

The McIlhenny home dominates the crest of Mayward Hill and, at the foot of this, there is a shallow lake, known as Willow Pond.

In the dense growth of buttonbushes which rim it, and on great, double-decker "apartment houses" of bamboo which have been built above its surface, some twenty thousand herons now nest each year and raise their broods.

Fifty years ago such birds had all but vanished from the world. Female vanity demanded "aigrettes" for adornment. These are nuptial plumage, which egrets wear only during the mating and nesting season. To obtain them, plume hunters had to kill the birds at a time when the death of the parents inevitably meant that their babies also perished wretchedly of starvation. The soulless slaughter took its inevitable toll. Too late the government made the mere possession of aigrettes illegal.

Too late? In 1898, young Ned McIlhenny, recently returned from the Arctic, went out into the swamps and marshes surrounding Avery Island. By dint of arduous searching, day after day, he finally managed to capture seven snowy egrets alive. Over the lake that is now Bird City a big flying-cage of wire was built. Here the seven captive birds were confined. For Ned McIlhenny recalled the story told at his father's

dinner table by an English visitor about a rajah who had built a cage of bamboo to which he brought rare birds from all parts of the world. The bamboo ultimately disintegrated; but the birds remained where they had been reared.

The seven snowy egrets in the flying cage were well fed with shrimp and minnows. Three pairs of birds set up housekeeping in the cage with one frustrated bachelor—or spinster—as envious audience. Three broods of young were reared in captivity. Then came the great experiment. The cage that hemmed them in was destroyed in early November and the released herons took wing. But the following Spring they and a number of others returned to Avery Island. And each Spring thereafter their numbers increased. Other birds share the colony with the snowy egrets. Occasionally an egret's hospitality is abused and then resentment flares into angry action. For instance, when an outlier invades a mother egret's nest, she defends it as best she can, while her mate flies to her rescue and their friends give a general alarm. Presently, the sky is white with wings. The outlier is ousted, the startled parent soothed, and the other egrets drop swiftly to their own nests. Then the sun goes down and Bird City is hushed for the night.

It is not only a metropolis, but a sanctuary—and a monument to the great man who founded it; a monument that enshrines his memory, more enduringly than marble, now that he has been gathered to his fathers.

"MR. MACK"

All through the marsh country, landowners have dug canals to take the place of the roads which it is not feasible to build and have erected levees on either side of them. Furthermore, they have constructed floodgates in the levees, to retain the fresh water in the marshes during the dry season, and to prevent an influx of excess salt water, injurious to plant life, during high tides. Sometimes, in the course of the rainy season, the marsh water becomes higher than the canal water and, when this happens, the floodgates are opened to let water out instead of letting it in.

Mallay Dubois, a trapper born and raised in the marsh, gauges depth almost by instinct; and in opening the gates he has more than plant life in mind: he is also thinking of the animal life which abounds in the marsh and on the canal banks— muskrats, otter and coypu—the latter generally called nutria, though strictly speaking this term should be applied only to the pelt. Dubois is no more of a statistician than I am; but he does know that Louisiana produces more furs annually than do all the other states put together; more than the entire Dominion of Canada. He is only one of thirty thousand who earn their living through trapping. Nor has he far to go in search of his prey. Within twenty feet of his floodgates ...

... his father, Rome Dubois, is already taking a coypu from its trap, and presently he will still its screams with a club, throw it into his pirogue, and take it home with the rest of the day's catch, which will include muskrats, mink, possibly a few raccoon and, with great good luck, perhaps an otter.

Neither Rome nor his son will ever refer to the coypu by that name, nor will he call it a nutria; he will speak of it as "Mr. Mack." For it is to that indefatigable naturalist and conservationist, E. A. McIlhenny, that Louisiana owes the fast-growing nutria industry, just as the world owes to him the preservation of the egret. In the late thirties he brought sixteen coypu from South America; in 1946 nearly nine thousand nutria pelts were marketed. It has been pointed out that even if that many "descendants of the eight pairs of immigrants were careless enough to get themselves caught in traps, there must be many others who were more fortunate,"[23] and the attitude of the Dubois' and their neighbors in regard to "Mr. Mack" is proof positive of their confidence in his future as a source of revenue.

243

WILD IRIS

Trapping is strictly a business proposition and men like Rome and Mallay Dubois earn their livelihood in the marshes where they live the year round. But in the springtime the marshland is transiently invaded by agronomists, industrialists, economists and other representatives of the more learned professions, who have come there in search of iris—not just any iris, though every Louisiana variety has its own beauty and most of these varieties grow in wild abundance throughout the marshy regions of the coastal parishes; but for outstanding specimens of those types most desired for propagation.

For example, a group, thus impelled, will take a boat at Intercoastal City, eighteen miles below Abbeville on the Vermilion River, and cruise slowly along the banks, with eyes peeled for the occasional iris which serves as a signal that farther from the shore the parent "colony" probably will be found. The explorers will then disembark and, walking some fifty or sixty feet apart, wade through the moccasin-infested marsh until they come to the iris bed, which may cover several acres. (According to Dr. George Arcenaux, a plant geneticist of the Department of Agriculture, the largest "colonies" in the United States are located along this coastal area.) Here they select the specimens most suitable for their purpose, digging up the plants with a special type of spade which also comes in handy for killing moccasins and taking care to preserve the rhizomes. Then, after returning to their boat, they wrap their treasures in moist sacking. Not until darkness falls will they relax their search; but finally they will return in triumph to their own gardens, where they replant the prize specimens they have discovered in the swampland, nurture them with tender care, name them for their best beloved and experiment in the crossbreeding which leads to the development of magnificent new blooms. Ultimately, all this may result in a commercial product of general value; but the agronomists, industrialists and economists are not primarily concerned with financial gain; they are pursuing a hobby which affords an endless topic of conversation with like-minded zealots long after the iris-hunting season is over.

It is at the latter stage of their activities that I enjoy seeing them and their iris. So long as moccasins are mixed up with their metier, I greatly prefer to await the results of it on my own gallery, where I can look out on beautiful bloom without the prospect of finding snakes in my private paradise.

244

SWAMP HOUSE

A typical swamp house is built on piling. A trapper's boat is tied to these supports and his traveling begins at his front door. But his dwelling place is also provided with a long boardwalk leading to the nearest levee, where his horse grazes, if he has one, and to the platform where he keeps his buggy or his truck.

The swamp water is undrinkable, so a cistern is invariably an important item in his domestic equipment, and his doors and windows are usually screened to keep out the innumerable insects which infest the swamp. But, on the whole, his living conditions are pretty primitive. He burns wood in an old-fashioned stove and uses coal oil for lighting purposes. His walls are generally papered with pages from mail-order catalogs, and his floors are made of rough boards, scrubbed bone-white with brickdust and elbow grease. He has large amphibious families, and feeds them well on courtboullion, crawfish bisque, game fowl, wild honey, muscadines, pawpaws and other abundant products of his habitat, supplemented by vegetables from the excellent garden he plants in the dry season. He does not lack for amusement; he has a battery type radio, which is kept going most of the time, playing Cajun or hillbilly music; on Sundays, after Mass, he and his family join their neighbors for a "grand 'primidi,"[24] at some centrally located house, and sit around for hours, drinking coffee and "passing a good time." Then, on Saturdays, there are nearly always
. . .

246

JOLIE BLONDE[25]

Jo-lie blonde, gar-dez donc quoi c'est t'as fait.   Tu

m'a quit-té pour   t'en al-ler,   pour   t'en al-ler a-

vec un autre que moi. Quel   es-poir et quel a-ve-nir je peux

m'en   a-voir.

SATURDAY NIGHT DANCE

. . . dances.

The dance hall is a simple frame structure, a bullpen at one end, a bandstand at the other. On one side is the bar, stocked with soft drinks as well as with beer, wine and hard liquor; on the other side are the benches where the very old and the very young are ensconced. The women and girls enter, free, by the door between the band and the bar; the men and boys enter directly into the bullpen; and though they may have drinks brought to them there to allay their thirst, whether they choose to dance or not, they cannot go out on the open floor without paying a dollar to the collector who stands at the front of the pen, guarding its exit. But most of them feel the game is worth the candle; by the time the dance is well under way, not more than two or three are left in the bullpen; and they are the target of earthy witticisms from their more virile . . .

248

. . . companions, who are now swinging lively partners to the tune of "Jolie Blonde."
A violin, a bass viol, a drum and an electric guitar make up the band; and many
of the airs—for the most part French folk songs—have been handed down from one
generation of musicians to another. Nason Guidry learned these from his father; and
he and his kinfolk who make up the orchestra known as "Sons of the Acadians"
have been playing regularly to the same clientele for fifteen years. Its complete satisfaction is self-evident.

The dances begin about five o'clock. By nine, the hilarity is on the wane. Weary
grandmothers have begun to gather up their sleepy charges and watchful parents
have glanced toward their breathless daughters. By ten, the last truck is jolting on
its way back to the marsh. The last wagon follows after it. Finally comes the last
buggy. *Bon soir et bonne nuit!*

Section Four

BAYOUS

BAYOU HOUSE

IN THE swamps, the whole cycle of life is determined and governed by water. Along the bayous,[26] water and land between them furnish the motivating force.

A typical house beside a small, remote bayou has a mud chimney and a cypress shake roof. Inside, it is very like the swamp house; but its surroundings give an effect of much more openness and space. A split-rail fence, with a flat-bottomed boat tied to it at some convenient point, bounds the farmland on three sides; but the bayou forms the fourth side and the cattle graze to the water's edge and drink from the bayou. Behind the house is a barn, adequate for winter storage of crops and for the occasional shelter of mules and cattle. There is also a chicken house for the flock of mixed Dominiques. The pigs are mostly woods-raised, unless and until they are put in a pen for "stuffing"; but a small smokehouse indicates their eventual destina-

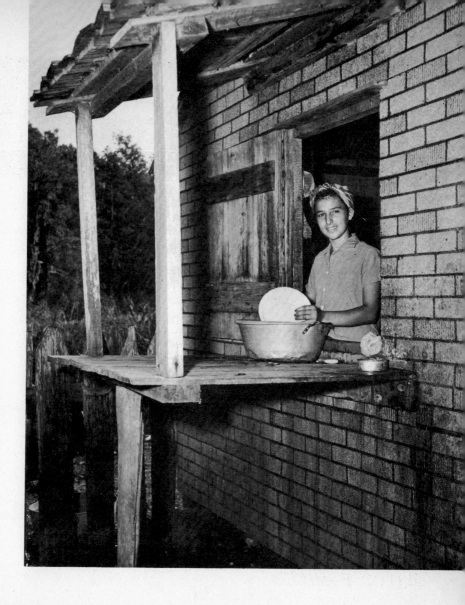

tion. Though the trees do not close in around the dwelling place, they frame it with their boughs; and though solid ground separates it from the water, the bayou mirrors the landscape from sky to greensward. The scene is one of the infinite peace that comes from seclusion without isolation and from the fulfillment of simple needs without the necessity of grinding labor.

Bayou families, like swamp families, are large and, from a tender age, the children are expected and trained to make themselves useful, the tasks which are suitable for each sex being clearly defined. The girls help their mothers with the housework and with the "yard chores." But even the former is not especially confining. A so-called *tablette*—a sort of window ledge—provides a convenient medium for washing the dishes and keeping tabs on the outside world at one and the same time; and when there is no valid reason for the *tablette's* use, a pretext can generally be found!

While the daughters of the family are thus employed, the sons work in the fields and . . .

BAYOU FAMILIES

. . . . learn from their fathers how to hunt and fish. The latter occupations are enjoyed; but they are also undertaken with a purpose. If a six-year-old can get a "frying size" catfish on the end of his line, it will later "grease the skillet" for supper; and the appetite with which he devours his share will reflect both his confidence in his prowess and his pride in his ability to help his father as a good provider.

While the six-year-old is fishing, his elder brother takes his pirogue and sets out for the store across the bayou. Most of the family needs are supplied on the home place; but it is still necessary to buy certain staples. The money to purchase these has been carefully counted out by *maman*. She will expect her son to account for every cent he spends; on the other hand, she is no penny-pincher. She will not take it amiss if he adds a few gumdrops and "Johnny Crooks" to his list.

On workdays, while the boys are fishing and shopping, their father is quite probably in the swampland. A number of . . .

254

ONE-MAN INDUSTRIES

. . . one-man industries are developed in the bayous—for instance, crabbing, moss picking, frog hunting, turtle and snake catching, shingle and crosstie making.

The bayou dweller who makes crossties has an agreement with a railroad representative to supply a certain number of crossties every month. The bugboat, which is operated in reverse fashion from a rowboat, takes him into the swamp, where he fells his trees and floats them to a ridge. He uses an adz to remove the bark and square the trunks to proper size; then he cuts these to the requisite length, loads them on his bugboat and takes them to the landing from which they are loaded for delivery. His "cash money" income from such operations probably approximates twelve hundred dollars a year and his labors are intermittent. A week at a time may pass when his most strenuous efforts are devoted to baiting a hook, playing poker and drinking coffee. Or he may go off on a hunting trip, which could result in a deer, but which will certainly serve to safeguard an unharassed way of life.

THE PIROGUE RACE

Bayou Barataria steals the limelight from all the other bayous when its world-champion pirogue race is held in May.

The pirogue used in this race is a special type, smooth, slim and reduced to paper thinness; even the bottom is hand-polished. When the race starts at Kaumer's store, four miles below Fleming's Landing, the width of the bayou is completely covered by the closely ranked pirogues, each manned by a swarthy, vigorous contestant, so tightly enclosed that he has barely room to sit down. As the starting signal is given, the dug-outs literally leap forward, propelled by the power behind the paddles.

For the first few moments, the line is virtually unbroken; then six or eight pirogues detach themselves from the others and forge ahead. Those left behind strive to catch up with them. Now and then, one or another of the valiants lets his muscle power get away from him. Like something out of a conjurer's box, he disappears from view as his trickily balanced craft turns turtle. Spluttering and furious, he rights it, fights his way back aboard . . .

256

. . . and digs paddle blade into the bayou; even the consolation prizes are well worth winning. A howling mob on the banks of the bayou and from the craft drawn up alongside it eggs the paddlers on, cheering the favorites; and when one pirogue makes the final dash and crosses the finish line, bedlam breaks loose: whistles blow, bells ring, bystanders bellow and sirens shriek.

The race is sponsored by a New Orleans organization of which Hugh Wilkinson is the head. He is also President of the New Orleans Opera Association. But, after all, this is Louisiana. Mostly the winners of the Bayou Classic are named Billot or Creppel. These are large families, and the Billot or the Creppel who is victor in one year may be only distantly related to the next Billot or Creppel to wrest the championship from him, while still another—Gran'père Billot or Gran'père Creppel it may be—crosses the finish line in forty-second place. But what of that? The forty-second prize may be two cases of beer—and you can't drink a silver trophy.

BAYOU LAFOURCHE

WATER HYACINTHS—A MAGIC CARPET

The first time that I saw water hyacinths in Louisiana I thought they produced one of the most beautiful effects I had ever beheld in my life.

With a friend, I was motoring back to New Orleans along Bayou Lafourche. It had been a day so full to overflowing of glad experiences that I would not have believed it could offer another. And then suddenly my companion swung the car onto the little bridge which leads from Paincourtville to Plattenville.

The sun was setting and behind the square tower of a small sturdy brick church, the sky was alive with glory. The reflected light fell on the clustering houses, the neat kitchen gardens, the lush growth of vegetation on the banks of the bayou, gilding them all; but nowhere did its radiance have the supernal quality that it attained as it spread over the delicate blossoms, which had the brilliance and color of amethyst crystal. Thus lighted, blossoms and leaves seemed to form part of a magic carpet.

The light faded and the spell was broken. Abruptly, I was told that the water hyacinth, as it multiplies and spreads does indeed, eventually, form a complete carpet, but that the magic it works is evil. "It hampers vegetation, blights fishing and hunting, destroys winter feeding grounds of migratory fowl, closes streams to trappers and others dependent on water travel. It clogs irrigation streams, and, by cutting their depth, causes damaging overflows."[27]

This is certainly a sweeping and damning indictment and, unfortunately, it is almost as true now as when it was written. At that time, engineers were fighting the growth with special boats which scooped the plants from the water and crushed them or tossed them onto the bank. To supplement these attempts at extermination, chemical sprays were used, and millions of dollars were spent in trying to do away with

258

them by mechanical devices. But, inevitably, a few escaped and these survivors swiftly multiplied again, until the carpet of evil magic re-covered the strangled streams.

Now the Army's Corps of Engineers has entered into a contract with Tulane University for the control of water hyacinths and other marine growths. Special water hyacinth laboratories have been established and eminent scientists have been called into consultation. At long last, the water hyacinth, which began its wicked work soon after it was introduced at the Cotton Exposition of 1884 as "a rare and beautiful aquatic plant," appears to be doomed.

But I am glad that I did not know that, as I gazed on it, enthralled, on an enchanted May evening, at sunset.

"THE GEM OF BAYOU LAFOURCHE"

The small sturdy brick church with the square tower, which I first saw at sunset from the bridge which links Paincourtville with Plattenville, has very suitably been described as "The Gem of Bayou Lafourche."

The parish of the "Assumption of the Blessed Virgin Mary" at Plattenville was established in 1793, during the Spanish Colonial regime, at approximately the same time as the Diocese of Louisiana. Its founders were a group of Spanish officials and a Spanish Capuchin friar by the name of Bernardo de Deva. The first church was, reputedly, little more than a shack; but its annals of births, deaths, marriages and baptisms, preserved in great vellum-bound volumes, constitute a record which is rich and vivid from the beginning.

The second church, which was considerably more pretentious, was dedicated in 1819; but this was destroyed in a flood so violent that no trace of the building was found after the waters subsided. The present parish church dates back only to 1856 and cannot, therefore, compare in antiquity with many other ecclesiastical buildings in Louisiana; but in atmosphere and in appointments it has few rivals. Its golden candelabra and chandeliers; the murals which adorn its walls; the magnificent carpet which covers its sanctuary; the superb vestments which have been preserved for great occasions; the sumptuous statue of St. Faustine and the relic enshrined with it—all these are unmistakable evidences of a rich and glowing past.

Many of these treasures undoubtedly came from France, for the French influence has been dominant many years now, as the memorial inscriptions on the stained glass windows and the legends on the Stations of the Cross plainly reveal. But there is still something Spanish in the feeling of the place, almost as if that first zealous young Capuchin had left a permanent stamp upon it. As a matter of fact, it would be strange if he had not. Though most of the Spanish missionary friars returned to their mother country at the end of the Spanish Colonial regime, Father de Deva remained at his post, became a secular priest and continued to serve the Lafourche section for many years. As a young friar he had the honor of receiving his countryman, Penalver y Cardenas, the first Bishop of Louisiana, in his parish; since then, every Bishop of the Diocese, following the example of Penalver, has visited it and officiated for its people; and, during the last hundred years, every Archbishop of New Orleans has done likewise. All have been appropriately received. Perhaps de Deva builded better than he knew. Or perhaps he was confident all the time that the future of his parish would be worthy of its past.

RIENZI—FIT FOR A QUEEN

The splendors of the Church of the Assumption at Plattenville lead the visitor to conclude that there must have been much luxury of living along Bayou Lafourche. The conclusion would be correct. Another striking example is Rienzi Plantation house.

This was built near the close of the eighteenth century, allegedly under instructions from Queen Maria Louisa—according to some authorities, as a potential refuge for herself after the Napoleonic Wars; according to others, as a gift for a favorite lady-in-waiting who contemplated voluntary exile because of an unhappy love affair. There is no claim that it was ever inhabited by either one; but it was owned and occupied, for nearly half a century, by Señor Don Ignacio de Egana, a former representative of the queen; and the Spanish influence, which has such a strangely imperishable quality, is still evident here as it is in Father de Deva's parish seat. A hallway, shaped like a Greek cross, divides the four great rooms on the ground floor of Rienzi from each other; and, in two of them, which could easily be thrown . . .

. . . into one by means of folding doors, the elaborate carving and paneling, as well as the spaciousness, instantly suggest the suitability of these apartments for state functions. Personally, I am very sorry that, apparently, they were never so used and I should be delighted—and by no means astonished—to discover that the house really does owe its origin to some kind of a royal romance! And at least it owes its name to the great Italian patriot, Cola di Rienzi, the favorite hero of an early owner!

It is now owned by the Levert family, who use it as their home and as the center for busy and prosperous plantation life. During the Spring Fiesta, they open it generously to the public and their attitude to visitors is at all times cordial and co-operative. Though in one way Rienzi may have missed its destiny, it has fulfilled this in another. It stirs the visitor in no way to feelings of nostalgic sadness. But very different sensations are aroused by a visit to . . .

WOODLAWN—"*SIC TRANSIT GLORIA MUNDI*"

... Woodlawn, which, according to old stories and old pictures, was once the proudest plantation for miles around. Despite the use of slave labor, the house cost seventy thousand dollars and four years of unremitting work went into its construction. Six magnificent columns supported the heavy cornice of the main building, which was two stories high. The connecting wings, simpler in design and less lofty, but effectively placed and exquisitely proportioned, served to complement the central façade. The walls of rose stucco, the capitals of snowy marble and the shutters of soft green blended as harmoniously as the architectural details. Inside, the house was not only splendidly decorated and furnished; it was also provided with modern conveniences to a degree unknown in plantation houses at the time of its erection in 1835. Gas was installed for illumination and marble tubs for bathing.

The first owner of Woodlawn was William W. Pugh, who achieved enormous wealth and considerable distinction both as a statesman and as a soldier. He died at the age of ninety-five, leaving fifteen children and a host of grandchildren. I do not know why none of these was able or willing to maintain this homestead; but apparently such was the case, for, a few years after the patriarch's death, Woodlawn was sold, and, little by little, its grandeur deteriorated. I am told that twenty years ago it might still have been saved, if any individual or group had been sufficiently interested in its salvage. This was not one of the houses that "the river took" or that "the filthy carpetbaggers despoiled." Nor is there any tale of grueling poverty—at least I have heard none—to account for the loss that it represents, not only to Louisiana, but to the world. Such houses were the monuments of a bygone civilization, no less than Roman amphitheaters and Gothic churches. Therefore, to the onlooker who is an outsider, the abandonment of Woodlawn seems all the more tragic.

When I first saw it, in 1942, the main building was still standing, though empty; hay was stored in the noble apartments of the wings and one forlorn Negro, who could hardly have been designated as a caretaker, was puttering aimlessly about the grounds. When I last saw it, early in 1949, the main building was gone completely and the great columns were strewn, in fragments, where smooth lawns had once led to the magnificent portico.

I know that I shall never go there again. I want my wanderings to be happy. A sight as sad as this one haunts me.

THE JAIL WITH THE WIDE-OPEN DOOR

The road which borders Bayou Lafourche has been called "the longest village street in the world." From Donaldsonville to Golden Meadows—a distance of about one hundred miles—no house is more than "two hoots and a holler" away from its nearest neighbor. Every now and then the houses cluster more closely together and a few public buildings appear in their midst. Then the village street temporarily becomes a town—deeply shaded, carefully tended, patently prosperous, slightly sleepy, infinitely charming. One of the most charming is Napoleonville. This being a parish seat, has one feature most others lack—a jail.

To be sure, there is usually no one in the jail—that is, there are no prisoners, except for an occasional brawler or drunkard. But there is a jailer, who raises vegetables and flowers and stays around—just in case. He and his wife live in a cheerful six-room apartment on the ground floor. This has iron bars on the windows, but otherwise there is nothing to suggest its somewhat ominous location; and it is a matter of pride to its occupants that its front door is always wide open!

266

THE ROLLING STORES

In the old days, shopping was something of a problem along Lafourche. It took time to go to town. So, as it was hard for people to get to the stores, the custom arose of having the stores go to the people. Now that it takes no time at all to dash from one end of the bayou to the other, the custom still prevails. It has become a habit as hard to break as that of taking drugs.

The rolling stores were originally primitive, horse-drawn wagons, supplying merely the barest necessities, together with a few gaudy gimcracks and staple sweetmeats to attract feminine and juvenile trade. Now they are high-powered motor vehicles, often painted bright yellow. And the housewife can buy almost anything in reason from the well-stocked shelves.

I do not blame the Lafourchais for clinging to the custom of doing their shopping this way. I think myself that it is infinitely more fun to climb into a bus than to go trudging through a department store.

A HUNDRED YEARS ON BAYOU LAFOURCHE

I have not meant to imply, by twice referring to the graciousness of living along Bayou Lafourche, that all the houses which border the longest village street in the world are large or pretentious. On the contrary, many of them are of modest dimensions, including the one in which the great Chief Justice, Edward Douglas White, first saw the light of day. Many others are small, humble, even shabby or rickety. But there are hardly any that are not shaded by magnificent trees and that do not have brightly colored flowers and flourishing vegetables growing around them. Sunlight streams over them and their doors and windows are open to the mild air.

One day when we were motoring to Grand Isle from Glenwood, the hospitable home of our friends the Munsons in Napoleonville, we saw a very old lady sitting in the open door of one of these shabby little houses. She looked so peaceful and contented, with her cat slumbering on the porch near by, that we were moved to get out of the car and engage her in conversation. She was quite willing to talk to us, especially about her age, which she claimed was approaching a hundred; and as various relatives of hers came running from near-by houses to join the congenial circle, they corroborated this statement. One of them . . .

. . . allegedly a daughter, proudly brought her birth certificate to prove that she was seventy-four. "I keep it handy all the time," she told us when we apologized for the trouble we had involuntarily caused her. "On account of getting my pension money. You never can tell when one of those fellows that hand it out is going to say you don't look a day over forty, and if you really are, you've got to prove it."[28]

We left the garrulous circle and the nodding old woman rather reluctantly, though we knew we still had much to see on the village street before we reached Grand Isle: shrimping towns with their drying platforms and oil fields with their tall derricks; fishing luggers with brightly colored canvas coverings; small secluded cemeteries adorned with shadow boxes; oleanders in a profusion of bloom along the byways and strange birds flying low over the marshland. Moreover, we kept on thinking about the old lady long after we had waved goodby to her.

A hundred years in a little house with flowers in front of it and tall trees shading it on Bayou Lafourche. . . . Well, that must have been a life worth living.

ALL SAINTS' NIGHT

The sturdy little brick church at Plattenville, which I first saw from the bridge, is the scene every spring of a festival honoring St. Faustine, whose regally robed statue is among the many artistic treasures of this richly ornamented sanctuary. On this occasion, St. Faustine is removed from her shrine and paraded along the bayou, under ecclesiastical auspices, accompanied by a group of little girls, wearing costumes patterned after hers and reviving the legends about her. In quaintness and charm, this festival rivals the celebration of the feast of St. Amico.[29] But for eerie beauty, no ceremony in which a bayou forms an integral part of the setting can equal the observance of All Saints' on the Bayou des Oies and Bayou Barataria.

In the "Lafitte Country" through which these bayous flow, the people bury their dead in great white tombs by the waterside; and when twilight comes on "Toussaint" they illumine the graves with tall flickering candles and keep prayerful watch in their proud small cemeteries throughout the night. The first candles are lighted without any signal except the instinct of the worshippers that now is the time. No formalities begin the rite. One by one the lights flicker into being. A breeze over the bayou fans the minute flames, giving them visible life. Night, falling suddenly, finds the beautiful scene complete.

The cemeteries are transformed. Freshly whitewashed tombs, which look bare and cold by day, take on new colors. Their façades are adorned by shadows, their outlines softened. A translucence like that of marble disguises the roughness of cement. On this night, the tombs of Barataria are as splendid as those of the mighty anywhere in the world.

270

Silhouetted against the white tombs, worshippers move from grave to grave, carrying more and more flowers, more and more candles. Not one comes empty-handed. At least one candle must be lighted in memory of every kinsman and every friend who has gone on ahead, by those left behind. Death and the ceremonies of those remembering the dead are not austere mysteries to these celebrants, but intimate and friendly rites of communion with well-remembered friends whose lives continue in another world.

Dead? They are not dead. They live in the community they helped to hew out of the wilderness, in generations of children reared to useful citizenship, in the blessed freedom they defended through the centuries with their blood. And they will always live in the pilgrimage of undying remembrance, made on this day of every year, to the silent cities, briefly aglow with light.

THE GREAT RIVER

THE MIDAS TOUCH

NEAR THE northeast boundary of Louisiana, the Mississippi winds on its way to the Gulf in a series of great, tortuous loops. But its swift current, constantly seeking a more direct route, occasionally cuts across the narrow neck of a loop, so that many of these now form lakes shaped like oxbows, some of them entirely closed and some of them open at one end. The land thus embraced is as rich as any in the world; for thousands of years, Ol' Man River, in each flood season, has been bringing down tons of rich soil from his upper regions and depositing them here. The lakes themselves furnish water for the cattle which graze on the lush land, and abundant sport and recreation, not only for the people who live near by, but for hundreds of visitors.

Among the great plantations fortunately located in this region are Lake Grove and Evergreen, the plantations of the David Lides, to whom we have already referred in connection with their fine herds. These plantations form a cattle empire in themselves, but they owe their origin as such to Mr. Lide's predilection for sport. It was this way:

274

David Lide is one of the favorites of fortune who appears to have been endowed with the Midas touch. A Tennessean by birth, he launched his career in the oil fields of Texas as a roughneck—the technical designation for those employed on a drilling rig. His rise was rapid. He became drilling superintendent, production superintendent, acquired his own drilling rigs, built pipe lines, wildcatted successfully for new producers.

In the middle nineteen-thirties, looking around for a place where he might hunt and fish, he rented a lodge on Lake Bruin. Enchanted by the idyllic surroundings, he bought it, along with a six-hundred-and-fifty-acre tract of land, and expanded this into an eight-thousand-acre estate.

But he and his son could not let Lake Grove lie idle, so they planted cotton, successfully. To utilize still more of the land, they experimented with Hereford cattle, and then abandoned these, on the advice of the Klebergs of the fabulous King Ranch in Texas, in favor of Santa Gertrudis and Brahma strains. It has all been highly profitable. In order to provide better bass and crappie fishing in Lake Bruin, Mr. Lide financed the construction of special seines with what is known as a game-fish escape trap. Gars, buffalo, spoonbill catfish and other species could thus be seined out, leaving the bass and crappie in undisturbed possession. But when caviar imports from Russia were so drastically curtailed by war, the roe of the spoonbill catfish sold in the New York market for three to four dollars a pound, their meat for sixty-five cents a pound, and the buffalo for twenty-five cents a pound, so that even the effort to provide better sport for the fly-rod, which Mrs. Lide wields as skilfully as does her husband, turned a handsome profit.

Lake Grove and Evergreen embrace a number of older plantations. Among them is Winter Quarters, so named because Ulysses Grant went into winter quarters there when directing the siege of Vicksburg. Another is Hard Times, the origin of whose name is now merely a matter of conjecture. Here De Soto landed, on his exploratory voyage of the Mississippi, and here he made council with a tribe of Natchez Indians before a stockade decorated with the skulls of those slaughtered to accompany a fallen chief to the Happy Hunting Ground.

Lake Bruin, the great oxbow on which both Lake Grove and Evergreen border, is named for the same family which founded Bruensburg, across the mighty river in Mississippi. There Andrew Jackson dwelt as the keeper of a small general store, and there he secured his license to marry the Widow Donelson. Near Bruensburg Aaron Burr was captured while engaged on a filibustering enterprise whose real objective is still a matter of dispute among the historians.

Jesse James and his band roamed the countryside where the Lake Grove and Evergreen empire has come into being. To this day one of the nearby plantations is frequently referred to as the Bowie Tract, because it was once the property of James Bowie, inventor of the bowie knife and later one of the Alamo's band of immortals. Tales of violence mark all the past of what is now so pleasant a land of peace.

Evergreen was merged with Lake Grove largely because of its prodigal pasturage. It included a great section of batture—the land on the river side of the great levees. This batture is overgrown with trees. Scientific forestry is now providing a perpetual cut of timber from the batture of Evergreen on a scale that threatens to eclipse the returns from the cattle which graze its lush pastures.

Just to make the Midas picture complete, two oil fields have been brought in on Lide leases along Lake Bruin. Apparently, the only enterprise that did not succeed was an effort to transplant some olive trees, which young Major Lide sent to Lake Grove from the Sicilian front in 1943.

Necessarily, the plantation is well mechanized. Bulldozers, heavy tractors, flame cultivators, chemical defoliators, power saws for clearing woodland, and cotton-picking machines are all utilized in its operation. But there is also a large field force, in addition to a competent and pleasant household staff, and the senior of both is Preacher—squat, powerful, laughing, and very black.

276

It is of record that he has picked nearly seven hundred pounds of cotton by hand between "can-see" and "can't" of a single day. My fisherman friends tell me he is the most skilful boat paddler in Louisiana. His feats of physical strength are almost beyond belief. So is his gentleness. A fawn, separated from its mother by sudden high water, strayed into his little vegetable garden from the near-by woods. He took it in and saved it from starvation by bottle-feeding it. Now mature, and known as Jimmy the Buck, it follows him about like a pet puppy. When he takes one of the skiffs out to the lily pads, Jimmy the Buck plunges into the water and swims along behind his adored master. Occasionally this necessitates strong measures, for when Preacher is setting out for "The Buzzard Roost"—a cluster of cypresses growing island-like from the water at one point, where the bass fishing is often spectacularly rewarding— Jimmy might try to follow unless well confined.

Preacher is also a musician of local renown. His instrument is what he calls a harp. To me the thought of this iron-muscled, squat field hand seated by a great, golden harp was indescribably appealing, and I asked that it be produced. Enormously pleased, Preacher obligingly reached into the pocket of his jeans and brought forth a shiny mouth organ. It developed that this was his "ha'p." One of his special instrumentations is the representation—it is more than an imitation—of a train approaching, passing and receding.

Preacher really antedates the Lides at Lake Grove. He was established there as a retainer by Judge Jeff Snyder, from whom the original hunting lodge was purchased. Apparently, Preacher at Lake Grove, like Jack at the Cottage, went with the place.

SYCAMORE ON THE BATTURE

As the river changes its course, it builds up land on one side, while sweeping it away from the other. This built up land lies between the levee and the river bed. Like all other land so situated, it is known as the batture and automatically belongs to the owners of the property on the other side of the levee. But it is often pre-empted by squatters, who are known as batture dwellers and who take their chances of being rudely dispossessed, either by the rightful owners or by the river. They live in everything from packing boxes to houseboats and earn a precarious livelihood by fishing, hunting and the sale of driftwood. They also help themselves to any natural products of the batture and sometimes this lagniappe acreage has considerable value. There is a fine pecan grove on the batture opposite the Cottage and a growth like this is by no means uncommon. Cottonwood, willow and poplar also thrive on such areas, converting them into profitable timberland.

Among other trees, the sycamore is noteworthy, though not from the standpoint of lumber, for it has little or no value as such. But its growth often attains a diameter of four feet and it towers above the other trees. The upper part of its trunk and its upper limbs are stark bone-white and are visible against a clear blue sky from a distance of several miles. Consequently, sycamores are highly valued as landmarks by hunters, fishermen and river pilots.

278

FISHING IN FALSE RIVER

The chain of lakes at the extreme northeast are not the only ones formed by loops in the great river; about a hundred miles farther south are Lake Raccourci and False River, which provide much the same fertility and much the same types of sport. Mr. Gordon Bargas of Baton Rouge regards large-mouth bass fishing in False River as a serious occupation; for several years he has been a competitor for top honors in fishing rodeos and quite often has walked off with these. Prizes amounting to twelve hundred dollars are offered by local sporting goods houses for the largest fish caught in these waters within a given time. In August of '49, Mr. Bargas was leading with a bass weighing six pounds and ten ounces.

SCOTLANDVILLE—A REWARDING
EXPERIENCE IN EDUCATION

On the high bluff above the river, a short distance north of Baton Rouge, is located Southern University, with an enrollment of nearly two thousand Negro students.

This university stresses two types of learning: the cultural and the practical. Its vocational courses have the same standing as its academic courses; and the former include not only opportunities for agricultural advancement, with the benefit of thoroughly up-to-date equipment, but classes in tailoring, photography, printing, masonry and carpentry. The natural talent of the Negro for music has every chance of development; the university has a band, a choral society and a quartet which are all outstanding. It is co-educational, so it is offering the same privileges to women that it is to men; and it is reaching far beyond its own limits, not only through the schools for

the blind and the deaf which are affiliated with it, but also through the improvement of rural regions with which it has established helpful contacts. According to the *Times Picayune,* in 1948, twenty-four farmers received cash awards, thirty-one others received certificates of recognition, and twenty-three Louisiana Negro farmers who had repaid loans for farm ownership were also honored. "These people, with no formal education, have, in terms of what they have, gone further than you or I," Dr. F. G. Clark, President of the University, told his student body at the presentation of awards. These awards were given in the Better-Living Contest for Negro land-owner and tenant farmers, sponsored by the New Orleans Association of Commerce, the *Times Picayune,* and the Agricultural Extension Service of Louisiana State University.[30]

THE LEVEE IS NOT INFALLIBLE

As I have said before, I have loved the levee from the day I first saw it, both for its natural beauties and for the sense of unity it creates between the land and the river. In these respects it never fails. But from the standpoint of a protective wall it is not infallible; about once in twenty years it is allied with disaster.

The latest break occurred just above Baton Rouge in March of '49, very early in the morning. The normal, seasonal high water had already begun to subside; so this break differed from a crevasse, as the term is generally understood, in that respect. A portion of the levee, weakened by an eddy, gave way and, in consequence, the river flooded several square miles covered . . .

282

... with sugar cane. Fortunately, this area is thinly populated and there were no casualties. Moreover, at no time was there more than a three-foot difference between land level and water level.

Within two hours after the break, Army Engineers were moving heavy equipment to the scene, ably assisted by everyone in the area. By means of bulldozers, put into action on either side of the break, which pushed the earth out in front of them, a "ring levee" was constructed, which afforded temporary protection; this was reinforced by sheet piling, consisting of timber driven deep into the submerged soil. Within three days, the levee situation was completely under control; and though the outlying cane had, of course, been drenched through and through, the crop was saved.

HUEY LONG'S BRIDGE
AT BATON ROUGE

The bridge across the Mississippi at Baton Rouge marks the head of deep sea navigation. Above it, only shallow draft boats can ply; below, there is plenty of depth for ocean-going freighters, tankers and liners. This was the second span to cross the Father of Waters within Louisiana. The first was completed in 1936 just above New Orleans.

Plans for such a bridge had been drawn up much earlier. A constitutional amendment authorizing its construction had been passed in 1918. But due to War Department requirements as to its height above mean high water, the cost was so great that no practical way of financing the undertaking had been found until Huey Long entered the political picture.

He made short shrift of these obstacles once he had cleared his personal impeachment hurdle. A highway bond issue was marketed and all the railroads crossing the river into New Orleans were induced to sign agreements to rent bridge trackage in place of the rail ferries they were then maintaining. Vehicular runways for motor traffic were added as an afterthought. Huey took all necessary steps—he was a United States Senator by that time—to have the bridge officially designated as the Huey P. Long Bridge on all government maps.

But fate denied him the crowning moment of triumph. He was assassinated just three months before the completed bridge was dedicated.

THE DOCKS
OF THE STANDARD OIL

From the docks of the great Standard Oil Plant near Baton Rouge, sixty-six percent of its produce moves up or down the river by barge or by tanker. The barges move upstream to redistribute their cargo, which goes on by rail from Louisville, Pittsburgh, Cincinnati and other inland ports to its eventual destination; the tankers go downstream, through the Gulf and on to foreign ports without transshipment.

The cargoes are normally made up of the heavier and bulky products—gasoline, fuel oils, asphalt and lubricants; and in addition to the commodities which go out, crude petroleum is constantly coming in from marshland oil fields on small barge tows. The work of loading and unloading goes on night and day, and it is no uncommon sight to see boats waiting in midstream to get to the docks, or jockeying for position beside them. In spite of the congestion, however, the docks are much quieter than in cases where a different type of cargo is handled. Here everything is done mechanically; long rubber hoses take the place of stevedores. And as hoses can neither shout nor swear, the prevailing calm comes as a surprise to the onlooker surveying the scene for the first time.

THE SHRIMP INDUSTRY
BELONGS TO THE WATER

The shrimp industry, like the oyster industry, belongs to the water rather than the land.

It has several important centers: one of these is at Morgan City on the Atchafalaya, which supplements the Mississippi as an outlet for flood water and as a navigable stream. One is at Houma, on Bayou Terrebonne. One is at Golden Meadows, near the Gulf. And there are many others. These shrimp fisheries have national importance. Louisiana ranks second only to California in the number of its people who make their living from fisheries, and the shrimp industry accounts for most of this employment.

Besides the tremendous market for the fresh product and the impetus given the industry by quick freezing, there is a constant demand for dried and canned shrimp. The drying takes place on platforms, ranged along the banks of the rivers and bayous, and the canning is done in factories which flourish even in small out-of-the-way places. The departure of the shrimp fleet from any given point is a great occasion and even the urchins of the locality are so impressed by its solemnity that they bring the miniature luggers they have made to receive a benediction.

286

I once went to Chauvin, on Bayou Petit Caillou, to see the annual Blessing of the Shrimp Fleet. The little luggers—two hundred and fifty of them—had all anchored there the night before; this was so the fishermen could go to Confession at St. Joseph's Church before taking Communion early the next morning. When Mass was over, they marched together in formation, following the priests and altar boys and cross-bearer. Outside, priests and people parted. The priests took their place on the flagship, which was decorated with tiny fluttering pennants; the men all went back to their own boats, each flying the American Flag above its other bright banners. One by one the luggers slipped past the flagship on their way to the Gulf. One by one the pilots, without releasing the wheel, crossed themselves and genuflected as the officiating priest sprinkled their craft with Holy Water from a golden vessel. Never shall I forget the fluid grace of those men who bent their knees and those boats which glided down the stream in harmonious motion. Never shall I forget the sun's shining on the priest's golden vestments and the smile which illumined his face as he sent his flock forth with his blessing.

NEW ORLEANS IS OUR SECOND LARGEST PORT

If I had been asked, a few years ago, to name the second largest port in the United States, I would have said, unhesitantly, that it was either San Francisco or Boston. And I would have been completely wrong. As early as 1840, New Orleans was our second largest port, and though it very naturally dropped from its proud position after the War Between the States, it regained this with surprising speed, all things considered.

It is a freight port rather than a passenger port, though a limited number of luxury liners now go from it to various parts of Central and South America. But even these carry freight as well as passengers and so do the few trans-Atlantic vessels that come here. The volume of this is enormous.

More bananas and sugar are unloaded here than at any other point in the United States. Lumber is another first, with mahogany from Central America a leading item. Coffee comes second, and the import of this supplies enough for one-fourth of all the people in the United States. Newsprint has been brought in from France to relieve our own paper shortage. Animals come and go from every port of the world.

Besides the produce from foreign lands, immense quantities of grain come by barge to the publicly owned grain elevator in New Orleans from all the Central States, via the world's largest inland waterway system—the Mississippi and its tributaries, joined here by the Intercoastal Canal, which runs to the Gulf. Barges also bring down great loads of mined and manufactured goods to be distributed here—coal, flour, automobiles, furniture.

Returning, these barges carry molasses to the distilleries of the Midwest, where it is made into alcohol or commercial solvents; also sugar for the midland markets, petroleum products and baled cotton. I had a second surprise in learning that the inland tonnage now being moved along the river, to and from the Port of New Orleans, is many times greater than it was in the legendary days of "Steamboat Prosperity."

The riverfront is not beautiful, but it is well equipped to handle all this tonnage. The docks are bordered on their inland side by a continuous line of municipally owned trackage—the Public Belt Railroad—so that cargo is transferred from the vessels moored on one side of each wharf directly into the freight cars spotted on the other.

The new and aggressive spirit, which New Orleans has applied to the increase of its commerce, also has resulted in the establishment here of the second free port in the United States, the first having been opened at New York. It is a fenced area into which foreign goods can be brought duty free. Here they can be packaged, processed, or otherwise dealt with. If thereafter they are sent to points in the United States, they pay duty on leaving the zone. If, on the other hand, they are reshipped to foreign countries, no United States customs charge is made for their temporary stay on this soil.

Another result of the awakening was the creation of International House, a center to which merchants and buyers from every land can apply for information concerning goods they wish to purchase or sell. Next, the International Trade Mart was organized. Here American mercantile and manufacturing houses exhibit their wares to foreign buyers. A good many foreign nations also maintain permanent exhibits there. The building is aptly called "the show window of a hemisphere."

All this has found an astonishingly rewarding response. Postwar port business for the nation as a whole showed a marked recession, yet that of New Orleans—both in maritime commerce and retail trade—showed an equally marked increase. New Orleans has not forgotten how to play. But it now devotes to its work the same zest it devoted aforetimes to diversion.

New Orleans is also the United States Army's largest permanent Port of Embarkation. Almost directly across the river from the Army's Port, is a great Naval Repair Base in "Algiers"—the section of New Orleans on the west bank of the Mississippi. Although part and parcel of New Orleans, it is rarely called by any other name than the one it has borne almost from the city's beginnings. Across the water from France lies Algiers. So, the first French settlers in New Orleans, homesick, no doubt, gave the same name to the section which lay across the water from them.

AND NOW THE LAND BELONGS TO THE RIVER

Above New Orleans, the river belong to the land; below it, the land belongs to the river. This is Deep Delta Country, which should not be confused with the large area in the state of Mississippi, generally called the Delta, and somewhat better known than this section of Louisiana, which, in my opinion, is one of its most fascinating. It comprises two parishes,[31] St. Bernard and Plaquemine, neither of which contains a single incorporated town.

If you are headed first to Port Sulphur, as I generally am, you have your choice of two roads. The one on the right bank of the river is a little the shorter of the two, and takes you past Belle Chasse, the handsome ante-bellum home of Judah P. Benjamin. However, the road on the left bank is my usual choice. It too brings history tellingly into the present, for it passes the Chalmette Battle Field and the Pakenham Oaks. But that is not the main reason I am so fond of it. I love its nearness to the levee, which is much lower than the levee farther north, and therefore gives a greater sense of unity with the river. I love the little beacons, rising white above its verdure and, after nightfall, blinking cheerfully through the darkness. I love its abundant wild-flowers, spider lilies and honeysuckle and iris. The thistles, which bloom at the same time, are beautiful too. And the scent of orange blossoms is in the air, for we have begun to see scattered groves though the road is not lined with them yet. But it is a lovely road all the way.

We are headed farther down the river, so we must take the ferry at Pointe à la Hache, for, on the east bank, the road goes only a few miles below there; but we cannot resist the temptation of making a stop at the Beshels' place, before we cross over. This is an unpretentious plant, that combines a small factory, which turns out nothing except plain cedar chests and wardrobes, with a large farm, well stocked with cattle; but it is an almost perfect example of the prosperity and well-being which can be achieved through a wise combination of industry and agriculture. A father and son . . .

292

. . . ably assisted by their respective wives, who live in a commodious and well-equipped house, own and operate the place; and all thirty employees come from the immediate neighborhood. The ample lumber racked in the yard is impressive in its quantity, symmetrical in its appearance and delightful in its fragrance. The same fragrance pervades the factory, which is clean as a whistle and provided with almost every modern device to facilitate labor and expedite production. The stockroom is small, the turnover rapid; the output is trucked directly to wholesalers by jobbers who come straight to the door. The Beshels' responsibility ends when they deliver the goods in their own yard and financial returns are steady and substantial.

The farm consists of good grazing land and the barns are kept in the same excellent condition as the factory. Louisiana is a veal country; the calves which have been dropped in the early spring are marketable by fall, and are sold by their breeders to stockmen to be grown out and fattened. So the cattle, like the cedar, represent a quick turnover. Having seen the success of this combination, I am surprised that more families do not undertake something similar.

SULPHUR AS A MODERN MIRACLE

After we have crossed the river on the free ferry from Pointe à la Hache, we are about ten miles from Port Sulphur, which is to be our stopping place for the night—or as much longer as we choose to remain. The Freeport Sulphur Company, which has constructed a model village for its employees, has not overlooked the well-being of its potential guests. A staff house, constructed along the same lines as the attractive bungalows which it provides for its personnel, is at their disposal.

As we approach Port Sulphur, we see the village on our right and, on our left, the huge crane and carrier by which sulphur is transferred from the barges which have brought it in from the mine to the freighters which take it to all the ports of the world. The heaped stockpiles, the laden barges and the burdened conveyor are all overflowing with beautiful yellow substance, some of it powdery and some of it lumpish, but all of it glistening. Whether our arrival takes place before or after dark, we see these docks fairly glowing with brilliance. The mines themselves are ten miles distant, at Lake Grande Ecaille, and can be reached only by motorboat, as the intervening area is all marshland. In fact, the very establishment of this mine is little short of a miracle. Sulphur was first discovered on this location by oil prospectors, who came upon it accidentally. Its inaccessibility was such that grave doubts were expressed by the engineers who were consulted as to the feasibility of extracting it from the earth with any degree of profit. "But a decision was made to go ahead; the result was one of the most remarkable construction enterprises in the history of the South. Contractors inspected the site in rowboats; prospecting crews placed sections of picket fences in front of them to form bridges over the syrupy wastes. Men worked up to their chests in quagmires . . . and the mosquitoes and other pests became so bad that they could not continue until engineers devised 'blowers' . . . to drive off the insects.

294

"From the river edge to the drilling place a canal was dug for all of ten miles. At both ends dredges shoveled up sand and mud, which was used to raise wide areas to levels ten feet above their former surfaces. More was needed; complete new bases had to be provided for industrial operations to the back and for a large town site at the river. Tens of thousands of pilings were put in place to provide a firm support. Seventy-five feet long, they dropped unaided for forty feet before pile drivers had to be used to strike a tap upon them. Atop the pilings, heavy reinforced concrete mats were deposited, to create an artificial floor for the settlements. Today hundreds live and work in dryness and safety above the surrounding marshes. Unending quantities of the brimstone are melted beneath the marsh by the pouring of streams of hot water. Raised in molten form, it dries in jagged yellow mountains, to be broken for loading at docks along the Mississippi."[32]

Today the great derricks rising above the mines give these much the same appearance as an oil field and represent correspondingly great prosperity. The industrial plant of the Freeport Sulphur Company is one of the largest projects in the United States which is practically self-sustaining, and its products, like those of the Standard Oil, affect many different kinds of manufacture. Unbelievable though it may seem, without sulphur there would be no automobiles to ride in, no airplanes to fly, no newspapers to read and no movies to watch—to mention only a few of the general commodities we would be without. The home uses of sulphur include ointments and drugs, dusts and sprays and fumigation; while one of the most outstanding advances in the use of sulphur-containing medicines has been the discovery of sulfanilimide and its related family of sulpha drugs, which are very logically called "miracle medicines."

The company is most fortunate in its representatives. The one of whom we saw the most was the Assistant Personnel Director, Pat Colligan, an "Irish Cajun" from Church Point; he has most agreeable ways, and so has his wife, who, incidentally makes the best oyster spaghetti I have ever tasted. Sidney Broussard, also an Assistant Personnel Director, is another arresting character, a man who knows his own mind and is not afraid to express it. At Port Sulphur they love to tell the story of a new preacher, more aggressive than tactful, who accosted Mr. Broussard in a café. "Are you a Christian?" he inquired brusquely. . . . "No," his victim replied, "I am a Broussard."[33] . . . "Wouldn't you like to work for the Lord?" the preacher went on. . . . "Well," Mr. Broussard answered, "I have a good job right now with the Freeport Sulphur Company." . . . "Well, anyway, won't you come to see my church?" persisted the preacher. . . . "I have just barely enough gas to get home," replied Broussard, and took his precipitate departure.

THE OYSTERMAN'S LIFE HAS COMPENSATIONS

From Grande Ecaille it is an easy run by motorboat to the oyster camps a few miles down the bay, and one afternoon we gladly fell in with Pat Colligan's suggestion that we should go to see them.

There are several of these oyster camps, sturdily built, neatly painted and surrounded by finely ground oyster shells from which luxuriant fig trees surprisingly spring. The one we visited had running water, was electrically lighted and comfortably furnished, and boasted three radios, one for each of its occupants, so that there would be no dispute about programs. We were hospitably received by the Slavonian owners, who immediately prepared coffee for us and insisted on having us sample the oysters which were being culled by a cheery old man, who worked with amazing speed and dexterity, on the lugger tied to the wharf. These oysters, opened on the spot and presented to us without artificial seasoning, were the most delicious I have ever eaten; their taste was as different from that of the commercial product as that of new garden peas from a canned variety.

The oysterman's industry is often profitable enough to permit the possession of a good car and a supplementary residence at which he can stay when he goes to town for intermittent shopping and distractions; but his life is generally considered a hard one and it is certainly a lonely one. He can obtain wild oysters from the coastal reefs, but they do not command a good price and it is difficult to procure them; so he usually prefers to have a "farm." To achieve this, he conveys empty oyster shells to selected breeding grounds, where they are systematically scattered to provide a suitable bedding ground for the spawn. After two years, the "crop is gathered," the smaller oysters being rebedded on the same ground, the larger ones being carried to a bedding ground nearer the sea, "where they may fatten and acquire the delicate flavor for which the Louisiana oyster is noted. After a period ranging from a week to two months the larger oysters are tonged up again, to be taken to clean grounds, usually located close to the oysterman's camp. There they are bedded closely together, so as to permit rapid loading for shipment. Several hours before the freight lugger arrives they are tonged up again, measured carefully in a standard metal basket, and dumped into the familiar 1½-bushel oyster sack."[34]

A PERENNIAL GAME AND A PROVOCATIVE STORY

Of course we did not learn all this at once, but our interest in oyster camps and our eagerness to learn more about the oyster industry sprang largely from the first excursion instigated by Pat Colligan. On our return to the village, he suggested that there was still enough daylight left to see Magnolia Plantation, at West Pointe à la Hache, and we gratefully fell in with this idea also.

Everyone was going home from work by that time, and we soon found ourselves behind a truck which was transporting a group of men whose daily trek is between Port Sulphur and Pointe à la Hache, and who while away their time by playing a game of cards called bourrée. Night and morning they pursue their pastime, undeterred by the jolting of their truck and the rocking of the ferry; and if a hand has not been finished when they reach their destination, they hold it over until the next day. Their game has the same element of perpetuity as the dominoes played in Crowley.

As I stated in one of my notes—which means that probably you did not read what I said anyway—we have not been able to do more than give a general idea of the number and types of plantation houses which still survive in Louisiana, despite the deplorable condition into which so many have fallen. But Magnolia is so ideally located amidst its orange trees, and has had a history characterized by so many varied elements of daring, mystery and romance, that it has cost me a real pang to leave out a picture of it—because its present blank and battered state made it unsuitable for photography. However, it now belongs to one of the richest men in Louisiana, a shipping magnate and banana king with almost unlimited resources and a strong penchant towards philanthropy, as my neighbor, Father Vincent, would be among the first to testify. So I hope the day is not far distant when Magnolia will come into its own again—and that then I can write a whole book about it: about the two sea captains who owned it simultaneously, and whose respective wives acted as its joint chatelaines; about the visits which Jean Lafitte made to it, bringing his bands of brigands along with him; about the Governor of Louisiana who eventually bought it, and built a railroad so that his wife, who disliked both steamboat and buggy trips, could ride in her preferred style between the plantation and New Orleans; and about the "haunted" desk with the secret drawer and what was found in this when it was finally opened!

I listened attentively while Pat outlined the tales to me. But the day had been a strenuous one and momentarily my enthusiasm for both sightseeing and stories was tempered by weariness. However, after a good night's sleep, I was ready to continue the trip with zest, and we started southward towards Venice, stopping first at the "winery" of our friend Mrs. Lulich.

ORANGES COME FROM THE DEEP DELTA TOO

Ever since leaving West Pointe à la Hache, our road has been bordered on either side with rows of citrus trees—not only the Louisiana "Sweets," which to my mind are the best oranges in the world, and the Louisiana navel oranges; but tangerines, kumquats, satsumas and mandarins. If there were only more space to raise these, they could prove formidable rivals to the similar growths in Florida and California. The Louisiana product is necessarily limited by the narrowness of the land, but its excellence is slowly winning the commercial recognition it merits; and I am acquainted with no light American wine better than its fermented juice.

The Lulichs, who originally came from Czechoslovakia, were among the pioneers in producing this. I usually buy it in jugs, for I have found that thirsty guests consume it with great appreciation. But even when I buy none at all, my welcome from Mrs. Lulich is warm and hearty. She insists on treating me to a glass of well-iced wine and she gives me beautiful branches, on which fruit and blossoms are growing together, to take away with me, so that I may decorate my house as she does hers. It is a friendly gesture. But then, we have been friends for a long time.

THE PILOTS ARE THE LOCAL HEROES AND WE ARE
THEIR FORTUNATE GUESTS

Below Buras you may continue along the highway to Venice where it ends, or you may go there on the levee road which follows the river. This is not a *river* road, in the same sense as the one I have talked about before; it is actually on the top of the levee, which is wide enough for driving. On one side are pleasant little white houses, deep set in their luxuriant gardens; on the other, the great river, with ships riding proudly on its stream. On the piers are wooden benches where friends and neighbors go to chat at the end of the day's work. The pink clouds at sunset are reflected in the wide waters. And then the moon comes out and everything is bathed in silver.

It would be in the morning, however, that a pilot boat from Port Eads would be waiting to take us to the mouth of the river.[35] The cub pilot at the wheel, Leon Buras, Jr., is doubtless the envy of every small boy in sight, for we have now reached a region where "of all the callings . . . the highest stands for that of pilot. . . . He is the Delta's local hero, neighbor-who-made-good and village spender, all in one. His is a calling of pulse quickening possibilities. . . . For two centuries and a half, piloting has flourished with a special color of its own."[36] Our boat is one of the oldest on the river, having been in continuous service for seventy years. But it is steady and it makes good time. Almost before we know it, we are downstream as far as . . .

... Pilot Town, formerly inhabited by both pilots and their families, now merely a temporary abiding place for the pilots themselves. It is here that the river pilots, who have brought vessels down from New Orleans, and who will wait to take others back there, turn the craft which are going farther over to the bar pilots, who take these to the Gulf. The exchange is made, very skillfully and expeditiously, by means of a small motorboat; then the sea-going vessel proceeds on its way. Since we are traveling only as far as Port Eads, as the guests of the bar pilots, we make no change. But the shift is interesting to watch, especially when the motorboat is equipped with a kitchen chair atop its cabin, where the departing pilot seats himself, apparently completely at ease.

We are seeing fewer and fewer trees now and, at some distance from the river's mouth, we cease to see them at all; but indigo and Bermuda grass ...

. . . are abundant; horses and cattle feed on them with contentment and apparently with benefit. The presence of these creatures is another surprising feature of this Deep Delta Country, when there is no other sign of animal life except waterfowl. The horses are less plentiful than the cattle, but they are sufficiently numerous to be noticeable and fine herds somehow subsist on the narrow tracts, intersected by channels, which mark the approach to the Gulf. This territory, where the land and water merge gradually into each other, has peculiar charm. The first time I saw it was under the light of a full moon, shining directly in front of the freighter on which I was traveling to South America. Under these circumstances, the scene has elements of magic in it; but it is beautiful at any time of day or night, and each time I go there, I find new glories in it.

The through traveler lacks one great opportunity offered to the privileged guest of a day: debarkation at . . .

. . . Port Eads, and a hearty welcome from the bar pilots on duty and from such members of their families as may be vacationing there. In all, there are thirty-two bar pilots, all of whom serve for two consecutive weeks and then have an equal amount of time off. They are united in a voluntary but official association, own their equipment, and have a sinking fund sufficient to provide pensions for their members at retirement age. Their calling requires tremendous skill, long training, natural aptitude and devotion to duty. They must be able to take vessels safely through storm and fog, over shallow bars and through narrow channels, night and day, summer and winter. They are a keen, hearty and courageous lot and I salute them.

On the occasion of our visit to Port Eads, we were hospitably bidden to a bountiful dinner at Headquarters, and sat down in a company of ten or twelve, including the Station Captain, R. J. McBride, and Captain Mott, Captain Hills and several others. The group was congenial, the meal excellent; we would willingly have lingered over our coffee. But all the time we were eating, our hosts were coming and going in response to the schedule listed on the bulletin board in plain sight of the table and, before we finished, a . . .

. . . freighter passed the Station. Almost immediately, we were hailed from outside: a boat was just pushing off to bring in the pilot and if we liked we could go along.

It was a perfect day. The water was smooth as glass and clumps of water hyacinths, floating out into the Gulf, dotted it with their fragile emerald- and amethyst-colored loveliness. Over the blue sea, the blue sky closed down, masses of filmy cloud drifting lightly across it. Our boat leaped forward into a boundless realm of rare and challenging beauty.

As we drew up alongside the freighter which was putting out to sea, my companions watched, with an attention bordering on intensity, the swinging ladder and the pilot coming down it. I was more preoccupied with the people aboard ship. A few years ago, under similar circumstances, I would have been envying them; wishing that I were in their midst, with Magallanes or Hammerfest or Isfahan for my eventual destination—as some such place very frequently was in those days. But now my thoughts were entirely different. I was reflecting that all those poor people aboard were leaving Louisiana—and that I was going to stay here!

EPILOGUE

I am an avid reader of Ernest Hemingway, not merely because of admiration for his literary style, though in this I think he has no contemporary peer. The reason I read everything and anything of his on which I can lay my hands is because no author, either past or present, with whose work I am acquainted—except possibly George Santayana when he writes of Avila—can interpret either the substance or the spirit of Spain as Hemingway can and does. But nowhere do the excellence and the understanding of the interpretation seem to me as marked as in the twentieth chapter of *Death in the Afternoon,* though that is the chapter where Hemingway keeps voicing his regret that there are so many things he has left untold.

"If I could have made this enough of a book it would have had everything in it," Mr. Hemingway begins by saying. "The Prado . . . with sprinklers watering the grass early in the bright Madrid summer morning; the bare white mud hills looking across toward Carabanchel. . . . It would have had the change when you leave the country behind at Alsasua; it would have had Burgos far across the plain and eating the cheese later up in the room; it would have had the boy taking the wicker bound jugs on the train as samples . . . and it should have had the taste of horchata, ice cold horchata . . . and the melons and beads of cool on the outside of pitchers of beer; the storks on the houses in Barco de Avila and wheeling in the sky and the red mud color of the ring; and at night dancing to the pipes and the drum with lights through the green leaves and the portrait of Garibaldi framed in leaves. . . . If it were more of a book it would make the last night of *feria* . . . and why should it not have the cavalry crossing . . . a ford . . . if it is Spain? . . . but it's not in this book."

I am grateful to Mr. Hemingway and his publishers for permitting me to quote from this chapter; as I said before, it seems to epitomize the very spirit and substance of Spain. But though I have long loved that country, there is now another reason why I wanted to use these quotations: I also love Louisiana and I have tried to write a book which would interpret it to those who do not know it or appreciate it. Four years of intermittent work have gone into the effort, and now that my book is done, or rather now that the time has come when I must call it done, I realize how many things are still left unsaid. So I think I know how Mr. Hemingway felt when he wrote Chapter Twenty of *Death in the Afternoon*. I cannot express my feeling for Louisiana as wonderfully as he did his for Spain, because I am not in his class as a writer. But I want to follow the pattern he has set, in as far as it lies within my power to do so; because it is the best pattern I have ever seen for writing anything of this sort and the only one of its kind I have ever wanted to follow.

"If I could have made this enough of a book" it would have had the pecan trees in it. Not just the great orchards of Pecania and near Bayside, for instance; but the smaller groves at the Cottage and at Oaklawn and at many other plantations; the wild growth—almost as luxuriant as the cultivated variety—on the bottomlands; and even the one little pecan tree in my own garden at Crowley. These trees are the last to get their leaves in the spring and the first to lose them in the fall, and Louisianians have a saying that they have a wisdom all their own, and that you may be very sure, after the delicate green begins to appear on their branches, all danger of frost is gone.

Short as their season is, their crop is a valuable one, with a yield of some five million pounds a year; and it is one of those which the Negroes most gladly gather, preferably on shares. My own solitary tree furnishes all the pecans we can possibly use and more; and when I was at the Cottage I had quantities to give away. Besides, I was not thinking only of the pecans' value and of the table delicacies they provide, when I said I wished I could tell you more about them. I was thinking of the coolness the groves give, even on the hottest days, through their abundant shade, and the exquisite symmetry of the long rows of trees. Next to the moss-draped oaks, pecan trees are the loveliest in Louisiana—or so I think.

And then I wanted to tell you about shallots, the great fields where you see them growing and the old gray sheds where you find women sorting them and tying them into bunches, before they are trucked off to be marketed. An astonishingly large proportion of the commercial shipments of these "green onions" in the United States comes from Louisiana; from a comparatively small area of it at that; and they are another important product. But again, it was not so much with the value of a crop that I wanted to impress you. I wanted to make you see those rich fields and small gray sheds along the old road which runs between Thibodaux and Vacherie, and the calico-clad, sunbonneted women who are doing the sorting, and chattering meanwhile like a lot of cheerful magpies. It is mostly French they are talking, but not your kind of French, nor was it my kind either, a few years ago. I am proud because I am beginning to understand it and to make myself understood; also, because the women do not stop chattering any more when I come into the sheds, but make room for me to sit down among them and share their gossip, even if they will not let me share their work.

"If I could have made this enough of a book," I would have told you about the Easter lilies, which you must learn to call Creole lilies when you come to Louisiana. There are great fields of those too, mostly among the orange groves in the Deep

Delta Country. Can you think of a more delightful combination than that—lilies and orange blossoms? The growth in the Deep Delta Country represents another commercial product, for the bulbs are shipped far and wide; but you will find these same lilies growing, in smaller quantities, in garden after garden along Bayou Lafourche during the springtime, together with scarlet amaryllis and many other flowers; and in this locality they have been planted just because people love them and take pleasure in their perfume and their grace. That is what I want to do too. My garden at Crowley will not seem complete to me until I have as many Creole lilies growing in it as there are in any garden on Bayou Lafourche.

Then there is another product about which I should have told you and that is natural gas. Of course a gas field is not beautiful, like a pecan grove or a garden full of Easter lilies; nor is it picturesque like the gray sheds on the Vacherie road where the shallots are sorted. But it is vastly more important, for it contributes to the comfort and efficiency of thousands upon thousands of public and private buildings, at a cost which is almost unbelievably low for value received. The largest known gas field in the world is near Monroe in North Louisiana and it was accidentally discovered in a rather interesting way: a Russian emigrant, whose name had been Americanized to Louis Lock and who had spent some time in the Rumanian oil fields before coming to El Dorado, Arkansas, as a plumber, secured a contract to install plumbing in the courthouse at Bastrop and in a church at Monroe. As he commuted back and forth between these two points, he noticed the lumpy land formation, which reminded him of a similar terrain he had seen in Rumania, and he became convinced there was oil in "them thar" fields. Then he dreamed about a flock of white chickens, headed by a magnificent rooster who kept pecking at one particular spot. He felt sure that the dream was symbolic and that a well should be drilled where the rooster of his vision had pecked. Somehow he managed to interest his acquaintances in the project and they put up enough money—and just barely enough! —to "poor-boy down a well" as the descriptive oil field phrase has it. And in 1916 that well tapped—not oil, but the great gas field which still holds the world's record!

"If I could have made this enough of a book" there would have been a great deal in it about sports too. I never wanted to give the idea that Louisiana was a place where "the goodly fruits of the earth" grew in great abundance, but where there was not much to do besides working to cultivate them and profiting by them financially and enjoying them in a quiet way. On the contrary, Louisiana is a sportsman's paradise. You cannot climb mountains here and you cannot skate or ski or toboggan; but you can do practically anything else in the way of sports that you like. The Southern Yacht Club in New Orleans is the second oldest organization of its kind in the United States and has developed a special type of small racing sloop, officially designated as the "Fish Class." This so impressed Sir Thomas Lipton when he visited the Crescent City that he ordered his London silversmiths to execute a magnificent silver cup, for whose temporary possession all the yacht clubs along the Gulf compete each year in a regatta.

New Orleans also has one of the country's oldest race tracks, called the "Fair Grounds." Its public entrance is, appropriately enough, on Mystery Street. The gateposts of its vehicle entrance are two slave cabins, well over a hundred years old, and the infield is dominated by a group of giant live oaks around which the Creole gallants of the last century were wont to race their blooded ponies. Near by, two

310

great race horses—Pan Zareta and Black Gold—lie buried. Attendance at the races, with Saturday luncheon at the Club House, is one of fashionable New Orleans' favorite pastimes. But the smaller places have their races too. Quarter-mile tracks are common all through the region between Opelousas and Abbeville and, Sunday after Sunday the farm folk foregather and bring their fastest horses; moreover, plantation ponies are raced at most of the Parish Fairs, which take place in the fall. Louisiana Baby, who was raised by the Delahoussayes of Abbeville and whose name was later changed to Lady Lee, broke many records; another horse of note is Flying Bob, now rated as one of the great quarter-horse sires. Frequently, the jockeys ride bareback along the quarter miles and a few of these youngsters from the Cajun Country, where the prevailing masculine build is small and wiry, have achieved fame in racing circles. The Kentucky Derby of 1947 was won by a lad named Eric Guerin who hailed from Maringouin.

I have already mentioned the precipitate exodus of the male population from its natural habitat at the opening of the hunting season, and the assiduous attention given to the woods and marshes throughout the brief duration of this. Happily, the sportsman who is an angler rather than a hunter by choice is not so limited as to time. Fishing goes on the year round, and its devotees range from the boy with a cane pole and a can of bait in quest of small panfish or blue channel cats, to the deep sea angler who battles tarpon, crevalho or huge sharks. Besides the tarpon rodeos held at Grand Isle, the mouth of the river and elsewhere, there is an annual summer-long rodeo for the largest tarpon caught within the city limits of New Orleans, which embrace at least a fourth of Lake Pontchartrain. For that matter, each fall the Commission Council of New Orleans passes an ordinance fixing the dates on which buck deer may lawfully be bagged within the municipality. Lest there be any misunderstanding, let me hasten to explain that the city of New Orleans and the Parish of Orleans are identical as to limits and that there are certain tracts of land in the marshes between Lake Pontchartrain and Lake Borgne—still within the city limits—where no man has ever set foot, except perhaps a stray trapper or alligator hunter. Indeed, some of the finest duck shooting in the world is occasionally possible from blinds along Irish Bayou, Bayou Savage or Chicot Lagoon, all of which are technically within the Ninth Ward of New Orleans.

I have tried to show you characteristic features of the State from one end of it to the other, but "because this is not enough of a book" there are still many places I have not shown you or told you about. However, some of these omissions are intentional. I have not taken you sightseeing, in the usual sense of the word, in New Orleans, because so many other writers have done that for their readers already. I did not forget about Jackson Square and the Cabildo and the Napoleon House and the cemeteries; I thought you were probably acquainted with them anyway, either in reality or through the pages of some other book. The same is true of Oak Alley and Madewood and Parlange and Rosedown and many other famous plantation houses, and of the Evangeline Oak.

Then there are some things I have not shown you because this is primarily a picture book and because pictures, for one reason or another, were unobtainable. For instance, there is the case of the escutcheons in the church at St. Martinville, which did not present the same difficulties, but they seemed comparable. This church is the only one I have ever seen in the United States where the sanctuary was adorned with anything of this type. The founders of "Little Paris" had placed their coats of arms in this holy setting, and a noble array these were, with ancient and honorable names surmounting heraldic designs. But for some reason the escutcheons were not replaced after being removed to permit necessary repairs in the church; and no arguments or pleas which we could make, either directly or indirectly, proved effective as far as such replacement was concerned. So, one of the towns which seem to me most uniquely charming—namely St. Martinville—does not have the representation I would have wished in *All This Is Louisiana,* although I have tried to make you visualize as many places as I could, for there are a great many in the State well worth seeing besides New Orleans and outsiders do not seem to realize this as fully as they should.

Besides the things I would have liked to make you see, if this could have been enough of a book, there are any number of things I would have liked to have you savor, both figuratively and literally; absinthe frappée, for instance, as it is prepared in Lafayette and as you partake of it there. On weekdays, you drink Bourbon in Lafayette, and if you are in any degree prudent, you do not begin to do this before seven in the evening, for even then dinner is still three hours off, as like as not. But on Sundays you begin to sip absinthe frappée directly after Mass, no matter which Mass you attend. "Sip" is the right word; you do not gulp it down. You drink just a little at a time, letting the well-flavored crushed ice dissolve slowly in your mouth, while you talk about pleasant inconsequential things in the midst of agreeable company. You can spend almost a whole Sunday—after you have been to Mass of course—like that in Lafayette. There are a great many worse ways of passing the time, especially if Fred Nehrbass has prepared the absinthe frappée. By vocation he is an architect, and a good one; but by avocation he is an amateur bartender, and one of the very best.

Lafayette is a great place for parties, which are sometimes held in restaurants that do not look like much outside, but which produce some quite marvelous food; sometimes in backyards, which are nearly all equipped with barbecue pits; and sometimes in the spacious dining rooms of pleasant, private houses. It is a great mistake to turn down an invitation to any kind of a party there, for they all have their points. But you are quite likely to find yourself at one kind when you thought you were headed for another kind. Once when my friend, Mrs. Maxime Roy, asked me to dinner, I hesitated about accepting because I was just recovering from a rather serious illness. However, I wanted very much to go, because Mrs. Roy is one of the most accomplished hostesses, as well as one of the most charming women, whom I have met in Louisiana. So I said I would, if it was going to be just the family. She assured me that this was the case and I motored over from Crowley—to find ten or twelve cars already parked around the Roys' house. But Edna Roy had told the truth—it was just the family. The Roys have six children, all married, and both Edna and Maxime have several brothers and sisters, likewise all married, and then there are all the cousins and the uncles and the aunts. Well, as I recall it, about forty of us sat down to supper, and it was a wonderful supper, wild duck and rice dressing and all the fixings. And I was none the worse for it the next morning either.

Another thing I wish I could have helped you to savor in Louisiana is turtle stew. This is entirely different from the clear green turtle soup, flavored with sherry, that you get in New York—and doubtless in many other places—and equally different from the terrapin à la Maryland, which is served in place of a fish course, after a clear soup, in Washington and Virginia and doubtless in Maryland as well, for obviously it originated there. Turtle stew, as it is served at the Hoo-Too-Shoo Club, on the outskirts of Baton Rouge, and at the Sam Tennants' house in New Orleans and doubtless some other places, takes the place of both the soup course and the fish course and combines the best features of both. It is succulent and spicy; you eat it with a spoon, but it is hard to stir, because it is so thick with turtle meat and rice and other important ingredients; and after you have eaten a plateful of it you decide that the rest of the dinner is immaterial.

Now there are not only the things I wanted to have you see and the things I wanted to have you savor, but the sounds I wanted you to hear, and that I would have made you hear if this had been enough of a book. I do not mean only the important ones like the sound of steamboat whistles on the river and the sound of Cajun French in the little sheds where women are picking over shallots; or the sound of *"Jolie Blonde"* at a Saturday night dance, and the sound of Creacy and King and Jack singing, "Walking to Jerusalem, Just Like John"; or the sound of the fountain trickling in the patio of Beauregard House and the tinkle of the metal tags which the dogs wear on their collars to prove they have been inoculated and all that and which announce their joyful approach in such a cheery way. I mean just the sound of names. Names of places: beautiful ones like Promised Land and Golden Meadows and Sunset and Mandeville and Violet and Vivian and White Castle; amusing ones like Blanks and Bunkie and Lottie and Duty and Trout and Vatican and Eros and Iota and Plain Dealing and Waterproof and Slaughter. Names of streets which may be divided into categories which bear no relation to each other: Abundance and Benefit and Felicity and Comfort and Humanity and Piety and Pleasure and Desire (which has no streetcar any more!). Then Euterpe and Melpomene and Telemachus and Terpsichore and Thalia and Venus and Calliope, some of which have undergone some strange adaptations as to pronunciation. And names of people: Christian names such as Arthemise and Theogene and Leudidine and Devince and Clafart and Araste and Palmyre and Eughlia and Demomine and Cloby and Clobule and Ulgere and Theall and Lianne. Surnames such as Claverill and Desselle and Sabatier and Blessing and Rabito and Copponex and Kurucar. The sound of all such names and many others is fascinating to me.

I hesitate to say anything more about my feeling regarding the neglect and destruction of Louisiana's great architectural treasures, because I have already said so much on the subject in the body of the book. Rather, I feel I should qualify what may seem like presumptuous criticism on the part of an outsider. Louisianians undoubtedly spend a great deal of money on their pleasures, which include the celebration of Carnival, the Sugar Bowl Game, the races and so on; but they also spend a great deal on cultural activities, especially in the line of music. Orleanians support an excellent symphony orchestra and a series of summer "Pops" concerts; and they are doing their best to restore the opera and the theater to the proud position which both once held in this city. (New Orleans had grand opera long before New York and so, for that matter, did St. Martinville.) They were zealous in their contribution to the war effort and when their interest is roused in any given philanthropy or charity, they are extremely generous. In several other states, the realization that the relics of the past had great architectural as well as great historical value came tardily. Perhaps it is only a little tardier here. I hope so.

I do not feel that any comment on Louisiana's "cultural activities" would be complete unless some mention were made of the great and successful effort to bring enlightenment to its most inaccessible regions. There are schools in the swamps and on the small outlying islands, and where there is no other way for the children to reach these schools, they are taken in pirogues. They go eagerly, even in the coldest weather, when they have to be wrapped in quilts to keep them warm. Until very recently, two little chapels, one Protestant and one Catholic and both built on barges, were towed through the bayous to provide opportunities for worship to those who could not readily reach a parish church. Now it has proven possible to minister to most of these people through small remote missions, though I know that at least one valiant priest still spends a large part of his time motorboating from one section of his parish to another, just as one faithful postman covers sixty-five miles of waterways in the swamps around the Lake Verette area. "Three times a week, Monday, Wednesday and Friday, he loads the mail in his boat and makes delivery to some nine hundred persons. Oufrac [the postman] has been on the same marine postal route for more than fourteen years and has missed only three deliveries because of hurricanes and other bad weather."[*]

The bookmobiles cannot penetrate to as many places as the motorboats, but they are doing a wonderful work too, supplementing that of the parish libraries, and I was deeply touched by the following story about a small boy's determination to profit by the one which plies in the locality where he lives:

"Failure to meet the bookmobile at its stop near his home in the Hundley community in Acadia Parish didn't daunt Shirley Francois or deprive him of his usual supply of books for the next two weeks. Learning that the 'library on wheels' would stop at the Acadia Baptist Academy on Thursday, Shirley filled a 24-pound flour sack with five books he had finished reading and took out on his bike to meet it. He made the three mile trip in time to be waiting when the bookmobile arrived about ten o'clock. Needless to say he went home with a fresh supply of reading matter."[**]

At least one of you, I am sure, is going to ask, perhaps a little sarcastically, "Isn't this enough of a book, so that you could afford to admit that there are some things about Louisiana which you do not admire or enjoy or even like? In fact, things that annoy you or displease you very much, which make you angry or actually unhappy? Certainly there must be, for no place is perfect. Are you going to pretend that Louisiana is a sort of celestial paradise in which there is no serpent?" Why no, I did not mean to do that. I really think it is enough of a book—though not as much of a book as I should have liked so that I could well afford to do that very thing.

But, in the last analysis, having willingly admitted that there is no perfect place, should we not also admit that though the imperfections of one are different from those of another, they are probably no more numerous? And also, though some are more offensive to us than others, this is because we have affinities for places as well as persons? A man who does not like a woman will dwell unceasingly on her faults

[*] AP News Features in the *Crowley Daily Signal*, July 21, 1949.
[**] *Crowley Daily Signal*, July 25, 1949.

and failings; but if his heart has been deeply touched and his senses strongly stirred, he does not say, "I would love that woman if she did not attach so much importance to dress—or if she could only discuss international affairs more intelligently—or if she were a somewhat better housekeeper." It may be quite true that she is extravagant or that she has no great grasp of world problems or that she is comfortably blind to dust; and he may realize all this more or less vaguely. But what he says to himself, with genuine feeling, is this: "I love her because she has such pleasant ways—such beautiful hair and skin—such a deep and complete understanding of my basic needs and desires." Or else, quite simply, "I love her," content to let it go at that. And if you do not see why I used this kind of a simile, there would be no use in saying any more, because you would not understand anything else I said either, no matter how much of a book this was.

But I have really written it because I love Louisiana, and I have kept on writing until I was told there was not room for me to write any more, if it were to be a book that anyone could handle with ease, or time to write any more if it were to fulfill most of its purpose. So now I must stop and I am glad to do so, because I have been writing for a long time and I am very tired. But I am also glad I did not have to stop before I had said this much. For "The great thing is to last and get your work done and see and hear and learn and understand; and write when there is something that you know; and not before; and not too—much after. It is not enough of a book, but still there were a few things to be said."

FRANCES PARKINSON KEYES

NOTES

1—I have three authorities for this statement: Lyle Saxon in *Louisiana: A Guide to the State,* Hamilton Basso in *Beauregard, the Great Creole* and Roark Bradford, who confirmed in conversation what the others had written. I consider Hamilton Basso's biography one of the best I have ever read and place complete reliance in it, as did Mr. Bradford, who was himself exceptionally well grounded in the history of the Deep South. However, it is only fair to say that some other authorities insist that Beauregard lived at 1113 Chartres Street only *after* the war.

2—A snowball is a favorite New Orleans confection. It is made of crushed ice, rounded into a sphere, dipped into brightly colored syrup and offered for sale on a paper plate.

3—Both of these houses are open during the Spring Fiesta, of which more hereafter.

4—Bricks reinforced with cypress joints, one of the earliest forms of construction in Louisiana. It closely resembles the Norman half-timbered style of architecture.

5—Quotes are taken from the Association's official booklet, issued at Spring Fiesta Headquarters. These are located in the Upper Pontalba Building, one of the most beautiful and historic structures in the city, and are themselves well worth a visit, because of their superb appointments, quite aside from the fact that they offer a year-round information service.

6—The present uptown section of New Orleans is, of course, much larger than the original Garden District, which, like the French Quarter, has well defined limits.

7—Webster's definition of a *veilleuse* (literally feminine form of *veilleur*—a watchman) as a "dimmed night lamp" gives little idea of its characteristics. It consists of a small vessel, shaped like a teapot, which fits on an open standard, the latter large enough to contain a short candle of the vigil light type, or a tiny, open boat-shaped lamp, in which a wick may be floated on oil. In bygone times, the lamp or candle served a dual purpose: it gave out just enough light to redeem a room from complete obscurity and just enough heat to keep the contents of the vessel warm. Though I first became familiar with *veilleuses* in Lisieux, they were once widely used throughout France—and, consequently, throughout South Louisiana—in the sleeping rooms of invalids and infants. A *tisane* was, apparently, the beverage in most frequent demand through the night, though milk, chocolate and bouillon also had their adherents. The *veilleuse* used by the great novelist, Honoré Balzac, marked with his initials, occupies a prominent place in his well-preserved study.

8—*Louisiana: A Guide to the State,* Lyle Saxon, Hastings House.

9—A "chimney builder" in Louisiana is a far prouder title than a stonemason. Many stonemasons cannot build good chimneys.

10—*Lafayette Pictorial,* March 13, 1949.

11—One of the best small-city restaurants in Louisiana is in Opelousas. The name of it is Didee's, and it is very efficiently run by a colored family, catering to white trade. It does not offer a wide variety of dishes, but its specialties are well served and superbly seasoned.

12—This, in reality, is the dormant pupa of a butterfly.

13—The Lides' Evergreen should not be confused with the plantation by the same name near St. Gabriel, or still another by the same name, near Vacherie. Apparently, the designation of Evergreen was a favorite among planters.

14—According to some authorities, production man-hours have been reduced as much as fifty to seventy-five per cent.

15—Bayou.

16—The first turn is just below Longwood, where the old River Road goes all the way around Plaquemine Point and the new cutoff avoids this.

17—"The Public Health Service does not list any of the discharged patients as cured since the doctors are not certain of that." Ken Gormin, *Times Picayune,* July 17, 1949.

18—I am glad to say that, at the time this book went to press, Belle Helène was in the process of reconstruction. Colomb as well as Burnside is in excellent condition. Lack of space unfortunately prevents us from presenting pictures of these beautiful houses and of many others which we would have liked to include. The author and illustrator have been faced with the hard choice between making Louisiana architecture the main feature of this book, thereby excluding many others, and trying to preserve a happier balance by giving a general idea of all Louisiana's chief attractions. We decided to do the latter.

19—The pulpy, strawlike substance which remains after the juice had been ground and pressed from sugar cane.

20—Ormond, on the River Road not far from Norco, is still another which has been rescued from ruin by private individuals. Mr. and Mrs. Alfred W. Brown of New Orleans have done a magnificent piece of restoration there.

21—*Louisiana: A Guide to the State.*

22—*The Sunny South, or The Southerner at Home: Letters embracing five years experience of a northern governess in the land of sugar and cotton,* edited by Professor G. H. Ingraham, of Mississippi (Philadelphia: G. G. Evans, 1860).

23—*Luxuriant Louisiana,* Baton Rouge, Louisiana: Department of Agriculture and Immigration, 1947.

24—Corruption of *grand après-midi.* i.e., a tall evening.

25—Irene Therese Whitfield, *Louisiana French Folk Songs,* Louisiana State University Press, 1939.

26—A bayou is defined by *Louisiana: A Guide to the State* as "a sluggish stream or natural canal, having its rise in the overflow of a river, or draining of a marsh." All South Louisiana is intersected by bayous.

27—*New York Times,* September, 1947.

28—In accordance with a law passed in 1948, old-age assistance pensions paid to indigent Louisianians over sixty-five years of age were increased to fifty dollars per month.

29.—See page 204.

30—*Times Picayune,* Sunday, April 4, 1948.

31—The geographical divisions, which in all other states are called counties, are designated as parishes in Louisiana. The word is also used there in its usual ecclesiastical sense, from which the other is, of course, an outgrowth: the church parish that originally comprised a small settlement gradually expanded its limits and the word parish became correspondingly comprehensive. It is also interesting to note that Louisiana is the only state in the Union which is not governed by the English Common Law, but by the Napoleonic Code.

32—Harnett T. Kane, *Deep Delta Country.*

33—In Louisiana, one family name is often outstanding, in a given locality, to a degree that I have never found elsewhere, though traditionally the Cabots and the Lodges have this distinction in Boston, the Adamses in Quincy, and the Roosevelts in New York. But I doubt if any one of these families numbers as many members, in proportion to the population, as the Moutons in Lafayette, the Bienvenues in St. Martinville, the Prudhommes in Natchitoches, and the Broussards in New Iberia and Abbeville. In saying, "I am a Broussard," the gentleman was making a declaration of great pride.

34—*Louisiana: A Guide to the State.*

35—George H. Peterson II, one of the Station Captains at Southest Pass, kindly arranged this trip for us.

36—*Deep Delta Country.*